CH00677872

ROBIN LAING is one of those lucky individuals wh‹ ests into a career. On the one hand, Robin is p most important export, her most successful tra greatest contribution to humanity. Robin chairs Whisky Society and writes many of their almost poetic tasting descriptions. He also contributes regularly to *Whisky Magazine* and has published *The Whisky Muse* (Luath Press, 2002) a collection of poems and songs on the subject of Scotch whisky.

On the other hand, Robin is also a musician. As a songwriter and interpreter of traditional Scots song, he has recorded seven CDs. Three of those are whisky CDs; *The Angels' Share* (1997), *The Water of Life* (2003) and *One for the Road* (2007). Robin performs his 'Whisky and Song' shows all over the world, thus being an ambassador for Scotland in the most enjoyable way imaginable.

Robin was born in Edinburgh and now lives in rural South Lanarkshire. He loves beach barbecues, star-gazing and walking in the mountains.

BOB DEWAR was born at an early age in Edinburgh.
First published at 14, and in print every day since.
Political and social commentary for *The Scotsman*.
12 books for Oxford University Press.
Illustrates for The Scotch Malt Whisky Society, Leith.
Married to author Isla Dewar.
Two sons. Two Siamese cats. One golden retriever.
No mention in the *Senchus Fer nAlban*.

The Whisky River

Distilleries of Speyside

to Alex

ROBIN LAING

Slainte Mhath!

Illustrated by
BOB DEWAR

Luath Press Limited

EDINBURGH

www.luath.co.uk

First published 2007

ISBN (10): 1-905222-97-1
ISBN (13): 978-1-9-0522297-1

This paper is manufactured from
woodpulp from sustainable forests.

Printed and bound by
Scotprint, Haddington

Typeset in 10.5 point Mrs Eaves by
3btype.com

Map by Jim Lewis

ACKNOWLEDGEMENTS

I WOULD LIKE TO acknowledge those companies that were helpful to me in researching this book:

The Benriach Distillery Company, Chivas Brothers (Pernod Ricard), The Craigellachie Hotel, John Dewar & Sons Ltd (Bacardi), Forsyths of Rothes, Glenfarclas (J & G Grant), Glenmorangie plc, The Glenrothes (Cutty Sark International), Gordon & MacPhail, William Grant & Sons, Highland Distillers (The Edrington Group), Historic Scotland, Inver House Distillers, Leap, Speyside Cooperage Ltd, Speyside Distillers, Duncan Taylor & Co Ltd, Tomintoul Distillery (Angus Dundee), The Whisky Castle, Whyte & MacKay.

In addition, there are many individuals who helped me along the way:

Bobby Anderson, Matt Armour, Mark Braidwood, Jake Bremner, Sara Browne, Trevor Buckley, Douglas Callander, Ian Chapman, Ricky Christie, Chris Conway, Neal Corbett, Georgie Crawford, Graham Coull, Sandy Coutts, Trevor Cowan, Ronnie Cox, Keith Cruikshank, Bob Delgarno, Bob Dewar, Mike Drury, Duncan Elphick, Andy Fairgrieve, Robert Fleming, Richard Forsyth, Margaret Gray, Alan Greig, Hans Henrik Hansen, Guy Heath, Elizabeth Hodnett, Darren Hosie, Gordon Jarvie, Richard Joynson, Libby Lafferty, Jim Long, Charles Maclean, Dennis Malcolm, Martin Markvardsen, Willie McCallum, Alan McConnochie, Ian McWilliam, Ian Millar, Ann Miller, Marcin Miller, Douglas Milne, Fiona Murdoch, Adeline Murphy, Martine Nouet, Jack Oswald, Lesley Ann Parker, Stuart Pirie, Alec Reid, Paul Rickards, Nita Rushi, Edith Ryan, Colin Scott, Jacqui Seargeant, Andrew Shand, Innes Shaw, Wally Strachan, John Sutherland, Douglas Taylor, Yvonne Thackeray, Ian Urquhart, Michael Urquhart, Billy Walker, Mark Watt, Alan Winchester.

I also have a debt to several whisky books: Alfred Barnard's *The Whisky Distilleries of the United Kingdom* (Birlinn) has been a major influence on this project, and Andrew Jefford's *Peat Smoke and Spirit* (Headline) was a source of inspiration. Reference books I have found invaluable include *The Malt Whisky Companion* by Michael Jackson (Dorling Kindersley), *The Scottish Whisky Distilleries* by Misako Udo (Black & White), *Scotland's Malt Whisky Distilleries* by John Hughes (Tempus) and *The Making of Scotch Whiskies* by John R. Hume & Michael S. Moss (Canongate).

CONTENTS

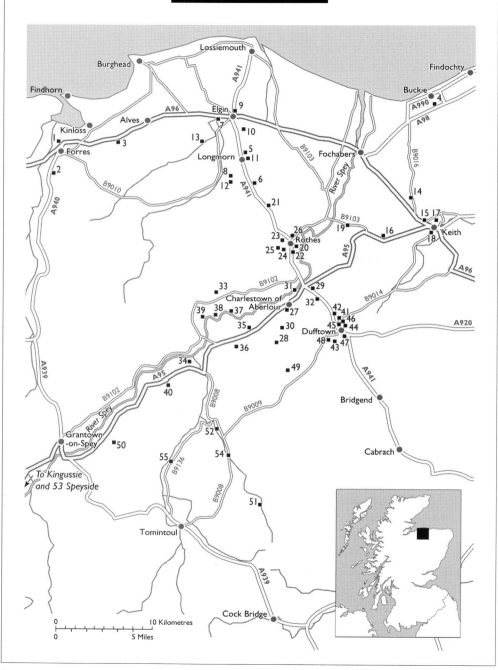

Key

1. Benromach *	31. The Macallan *
2. Dallas Dhu *	32. Speyside Cooperage *
3. Glenburgie	33. Cardhu *
4. Inchgower	34. Cragganmore **
5. Benriach **	35. Dailuaine
6. Glen Elgin	36. Glenfarclas *
7. Glen Moray *	37. Imperial
8. Glenlossie	38. Knockando **
9. Gordon & MacPhail	39. Tamdhu
10. Linkwood	40. Tormore **
11. Longmorn	41. The Balvenie **
12. Mannochmore	42. Convalmore
13. Miltonduff	43. Dufftown
14. Aultmore	44. Glendullan
15. Glen Keith	45. Glenfiddich *
16. Glentauchers	46. Kininvie
17. Strathisla *	47. Mortlach
18. Strathmill	48. Pittyvaich
19. Auchroisk	49. Allt a Bhainne
20. Caperdonich	50. Balmenach
21. Coleburn	51. Braeval
22. Forsyths Coppersmiths	52. The Glenlivet *
23. Glen Grant *	53. Speyside
24. Glen Spey	54. Tamnavulin
25. Glenrothes	55. Tomintoul
26. Speyburn	
27. Aberlour *	
28. Benrinnes	
29. Craigellachie	
30. Glenallachie	

*   distillery has a visitor centre
** visits by arrangement only

LIST OF ABBREVIATIONS

DCL	Distillers Company Ltd
IDV	International Distillers & Vintners Ltd
SMD	Scottish Malt Distillers Ltd
UDV	United Distillers & Vintners Ltd
ppm	parts per million (phenolic)
abv	alcohol by volume (percentage)

SPEYSIDE WHISKY SONG
(to the tune of The Road to the Isles)

ROBIN LAING

By Benromach and Balmenach and
*   Benriach I will go*
For the Whisky River's calling me away
By Tormore and Tamnavoulin, by
*   Aultmore and Tomintoul*
For a spiritual sprauchle by the Spey

By Macallan and Glendullan and
*   Glenallachie we'll go*
Distilleries unfolding by the score
By Kininvie and Craigellachie, Mortlach
*   and Auchroisk*
Pityvaich and Miltonduff and
*   Mannochmore*

There's a wee dram waiting at the end of
*   every mile*
From Dufftown all the way to Dallas Dhu
And a wee sensation that will surely make
*   you smile*
At Knockando, Caperdonich and Cardhu

From Glenrothes to Gentauchers, from
*   Glenfarclas to Glenspey*
From Glen Moray to Glen Elgin and
*   Glen Grant*
From Glenfiddich to Glenlossie,
*   Glenlivet to Glen Keith*
I'm a whisky-sippin' Speyside sycophant

There's Braeval and there's Benrinnes,
*   Linkwood and Cragganmore*
Then there's Speyburn and Strathisla
*   and Strathmill*
There's Inchgower, Aberlour,
*   Longmorn and Tamdhu*
And the only problem's picking up the bill

And the Spey runs sweetly from the
*   mountains to the sea*
Through scenery so stunning and sublime
There are angels everywhere, soaking up
*   their share*
Aye and that's OK as long as I get mine

For the heid or for the body, taken neat
*   or in a toddy*
As a medicine it canny be surpassed
If you're fightin off a lurgie, you can
*   gargle wi' Glenburgie*
If you're feeling rather blue then try a
*   double o' Dailuaine*
If you're miserable and fluish hae a
*   drappie o' Drumguish*
And for ony kind o' pain scoop a shot o'
*   Allt a Bhainne*
And Balvenie is Viagra in a glass

INTRODUCTION

IN 1887, ALFRED BARNARD published his book, *The Whisky Distilleries of the United Kingdom*. It was a massive undertaking, the result of the best part of two years' travelling and writing about whisky distilleries. Barnard was no whisky expert, though his knowledge at the end of his journey was undoubtedly greater than it was at the beginning. His work is an entertaining and well-written snapshot of distilling and the whisky industry in the 1880s. It is fascinating and of unique value to anyone interested in the history of whisky.

Barnard was very modest about his own work, saying, 'It is simply the product of a run through the Distilleries, with an endeavour to give descriptive sketches upon each in more or less detail.' The detail, readers find, is usually more than less and at times it can seem tedious and repetitive. Nonetheless, there is value in its comprehensiveness and in Barnard's intuitive understanding that whisky-making is fundamentally about engineering (which could be why the Scots are so good at it). It is for us, or for future readers, to pick out the bits of interest from the many carefully recorded details of measurements and capacities. Frustratingly, Barnard usually had very little to say about stills or casks, the very things that might intrigue us most today, but *The Whisky Distilleries* is, after all, a work of its time.

For me, the greatest value in Barnard's book is that he understood that whisky is about poetry as well as engineering. When he is not recording endless technical details, Barnard is eloquent and poetic about the landscape, about the history and about the cultural and social context of whisky-making. One gains insight into the methods of travelling around Scotland in the 1880s and his travelogue paragraphs are a joy to read, as are his anecdotes and stories. Finally, many of the entries are enhanced by a flourish of poetry or song.

Unfortunately, Barnard seemed unable or unwilling to use his poetic powers to describe the whisky itself, seldom mentioning it at all. This might seem strange to us today as he clearly did partake of the stuff with which his book is entirely concerned, but once again we have to remember that *The Whisky Distilleries* is of its time; describing the aromas, flavours and characteristics of various whiskies was not to become common until almost a hundred years later with the pioneering work of writers like Michael Jackson.

Barnard was visiting distilleries at an interesting time, 60 years or so after the

Excise Act of 1823 had sounded the death knell for illicit distilling and given licensed distilling a forward boost. Between the writing of the act and the commencement of Barnard's travels, the Coffey still had been invented and put into production, blended whisky had arrived and *phylloxera* had devastated wine and brandy production in France. It was a time of optimism for the whisky industry; Barnard frequently makes reference to exports, with one whisky being 'sold principally in England, Scotland and the Colonies, where it is of some reputation' (Balmenach) and another being 'shipped to all parts of the world' (Glenlivet), and he points out that whisky 'brings the largest revenue to the Imperial Exchequer of any industry in the United Kingdom'.

The whisky industry is always subject to economic and market forces that cause it to suffer from peaks and troughs of fortune. That was just as true before the writing of *The Whisky Distilleries* as it has been since. Just around the corner by a few years was the biggest boom and bust of all — that of the last decade of the 19th century. This had a particular impact in Speyside, where 21 new distilleries were built during the 1890s, just before the Pattison's scandal very nearly paralysed the industry altogether. It is interesting to note, however, that all the distilleries Barnard visited in Speyside are still in production. In no other part of Scotland is that true and in some other areas very hard times lay ahead, as for example in Campbeltown. This surely must say some-thing about the quality of the product from the Speyside area.

Barnard took on the task of visiting every distillery in the UK at a time when it was very unusual for anyone to visit distilleries at all. This may have worked in his favour. He tells us that 'Every where I was received courteously, and in many places with kindly hospitality.' These days, visiting distilleries has become a much more common pastime and this can result in a mixed bag of experiences. Either distilleries are geared up to receive visitors, often playing a significant role in the heritage industry, or they are not — and those that are not tend to be out of bounds to tourists, whisky anoraks and the idly curious.

Whisky is once again in a time of change. The growth in the heritage and tourism aspect of distilling is one element. Another is the growing appeal of single malts and the diversity of expressions of malts, including various ages, special editions and wood finishes. Around the world, whisky clubs, whisky festivals and tasting events are increasing in popularity and number in a phenomenal way. After the lean years of the 1980s, the global market and future survival of whisky now seem hopeful. However, many other countries are starting to make their own versions of whisky and one or two of them are disconcertingly good.

Distilleries have hugely increased production over the years and have tended to lose their maltings and their cooperages, preferring to buy those services in. Few of the pagodas (post-Barnard inventions) that are scattered around Speyside have smoke rising today. A growing number of distilleries no longer warehouse casks on-site. Rationalisation and economies of scale are as relevant to distilling as to any other industry. The sense of tradition evoked by many companies in their marketing is often sacrificed in the name of profit and efficiency.

Fuel sources have changed from water power, steam engines, peat and open fires to oil and gas boilers and electricity; transport has shifted from trains and ships to road haulage; automation, energy efficiency and stringent environmental requirements all of paramount importance. Far fewer people are directly employed in making whisky at distillery sites now but whisky still provides work for a vast army once you consider ancillary jobs and support services.

Have these changes impacted upon the taste of the whisky? Undoubtedly the biggest change in Speyside since Barnard's time has been that from peated to very lightly peated or unpeated barley. The modern whisky of Speyside will be quite different for that reason alone, though at least three Speyside distilleries are now producing peated styles of whisky once again. The change in most distilleries from direct-fired stills to steam-heated stills will probably also have impacted on the character of the whisky, as might the tendency to use condensers instead of worms.

Changes in wood management are obvious, especially the rise of bourbon wood in place of sherry and wine casks. On the other hand, whisky is probably matured longer in cask now than it was in the days of Barnard (for him, 'very old' is about eight years). Replacing wooden washbacks with stainless steel vessels may have had some impact, though that is debatable. Also debated is the impact of maturing some whisky stocks far from their places of origin; Chivas Brothers believe this does have an effect on taste and choose to mature all their single malt stocks in Speyside.

On the positive side, however, advances in chemistry, laboratory testing, training of blenders and samplers, improved technology and refinement of distillation regimes have all led to better quality control and a more consistent product. It remains true that whisky can vary from a relatively uninteresting dram to an ecstasy-inducing heavenly nectar but one hardly ever encounters a genuinely bad whisky. I doubt that could have been said with any confidence in the 1880s.

Whisky remains Scotland's greatest export and is hugely important to the government's revenues. Whisky distilling is the great survivor of the traditional Scottish industries; coal mining, steelmaking, heavy industry, ship building and fishing have all gone but whisky endures as Scotland's contribution to humanity. It also happens to be a passion of mine. I thought this not a bad time to visit the modern distilleries and report on what is happening throughout the land. I chose to start with Speyside, the whisky heartland, where about half of Scotland's distilleries are located.

I was not trying to follow in Barnard's footsteps or to do the same thing that he did, but I do take him as a role model and inspiration. I have chosen to follow his lead in some areas and take my own path in others. I mention the landscape and my travelling experiences from time to time, as he did; I delight, also as he did, in the history, stories and tales from each distillery and its surrounding area. I have gone further than he in the use of extracts from poetry and song as I believe they add something of value to the entries. I have followed his lead in describing technical aspects of distilling, though I have tried to mention equipment, buildings, plants and distilling practices only where these seem particularly interesting or unusual in some way. Finally, I have tried to say a little about the whisky itself wherever I have some experience to draw on, for, in the end, that is what it is all about.

One could argue that whisky regions are no longer relevant and that distinctive regional character no longer exists, but Speyside continues to have a regional reality for two reasons: firstly the sheer concentration of whisky-making in a relatively small area and secondly the quality of the produce; the top four best selling single malts in the world are all Speysides.

Most of my travelling was done in the autumn months, when the weather in Speyside can still be kind and the numbers of tourists is less. It has always seemed to me that autumn is the whisky season, with its golden leaves, smoky bonfires and the first chill of the year. Whisky can, of course, be drunk at any time and in any place; it is an amazingly versatile drink. Towards the end of autumn, much of nature is settling down for a sleep after the vigour of summer. The cycle of the seasons is echoed in the diurnal rhythm of our lives — and reflected beautifully in the creation of whisky, in which the tremendous energy of malting, of fermentation and of distillation is followed by the long sleep of maturation. Both elements — the energy and the rest — are contained within it and when we open a bottle we might either find that tasting it invigorates us or makes us sleep like babies.

The Speyside area is hugely rewarding, stretching as it does from the foothills of the Cairngorm mountains to the shores of the Moray Firth. It is steeped in history of all kinds, not just that of distilling, and I enjoyed my journeys immensely. There were times when I wished I could have slowed down to the pace at which Barnard travelled, but this too is a book of its time and the days of horse drawn transport and the Speyside railways are gone, at least for now.

THE LAIGH OF MORAY

'Laigh' just means lowland. The coastal strip of Moray is very fertile, having good alluvial soils, and it is said that this region gets 40 more days of sunshine than any other part of Scotland – great barley country. It should include Elgin, but Elgin is such a whisky hub that it deserves its own chapter.

BENROMACH
DALLAS DHU
GLENBURGIE
INCHGOWER

Photo: Robin Laing

BENROMACH

THE TOWN OF FORRES is on the River Findhorn, near the end of its journey to the sea. Just a stone's throw to the north are Findhorn Bay and the sandy beaches of the Moray Firth. There is as much historical interest in Forres as in any town in the North East. It also happens to be a very attractive town, with architectural charms and pleasant gardens, and has won the Scotland in Bloom title nine times. Just along the coast is Burghead, once an important Pictish capital and now the home of the Burghead Maltings, which supplies many of the distilleries in Speyside. The chimney of Benromach distillery is a well-known landmark on this part of the Moray Firth coast, both to boats and to jets from nearby RAF Kinloss.

The distillery was established here in 1898 by Duncan McCallum and F. W. Brickman and was designed by Charles Cree Doig. This may well have been the same D. McCallum who was associated with Glen Nevis and Glen Scotia distilleries and who committed suicide by drowning himself in Campbeltown Loch in 1930, thereby unwittingly providing part of the inspiration for the famous song, 'Campbeltown Loch' (I wish you were whisky). Benromach suffered, as so many distilleries did, in the post-Pattison's crash period at the end of the 19th century. A number of changes of ownership took place over the next few decades until it was taken over by DCL in 1953. In 1983 it was one of 11 distilleries sacrificed by that company on the altar of rationalisation at a time of overproduction. Benromach suf-

fered considerable cannibalisation — the mill went to Oban, the stills to Glen Ord, and various other parts flew to new homes elsewhere.

Ten years later the Elgin whisky merchants Gordon & MacPhail stepped in and bought Benromach from United Distillers. They spent the next five years carefully planning and rebuilding the distillery in order to recommence production in its centenary year, 1998. The reopening was marked by a ceremony presided over by HRH the Prince of Wales; cask number one from the new production was signed by Charles and still sits proudly in the warehouse. How long will it lie there and what will be its fate, I wonder.

It took Gordon & MacPhail five years to get the distillery into working condition because they wanted to take their time and get it right. When they took over in 1993 the spirit receiver was about the only usable piece of equipment left. They acquired a small reconditioned Boby mill and rebuilt four larch washbacks from what remained of the old ones. They had a 1.5 tonne mash tun specially made – the smallest in Speyside – and they commissioned two brand new stills from Forsyths of Rothes. They did not attempt to copy the previous size or shape of the old Benromach stills but rather created something that would suit their own preferred style.

The scale of production is the smallest in Speyside at around 130,000 litres per annum and the entire operation is run by two men. However, the philosophy is to make every effort to maximise the quality of the whisky. Keith Cruickshank, the manager, told me, 'If any practice or choice could make even the smallest difference to the finished product, we will take the quality decision.'

Gordon & MacPhail have built a huge experience, over many years, of cask maturation. They believe that about two-thirds of the flavour comes from maturation and so take it very seriously indeed. They use a variety of well chosen casks, for the most part first fill bourbon but with some American oak sherry

butts from Spain (they say that European oak can be too resinous). Barley is also chosen with great care; always Scottish, with a phenolic content specification of 8–12ppm, which is relatively high for Speyside. Finally, the wash is fermented very slowly (between three and five days) and distilled slowly and generously, less than 20 per cent being drawn off in the middle cut. This is not an operation run by chemists and accountants.

When Gordon & MacPhail ran out of space in their warehouse they decided to have a new one built in the traditional dunnage style. Nobody else would do that these days, but they wanted the casks to enjoy the best maturation environment possible and to take advantage of the

coastal position and the sea air. Benromach is a heart-warming example of a distillery rescued, thanks to Gordon & MacPhail, and is a good example of the 'small is beautiful' approach to whisky-making.

The visitor centre was opened in 1999 and already has about 5,000 visitors a year. They are gradually gathering the contents of a museum of distillation next door.

As no Benromach was produced between 1983 and 1998, there is a large gap in the stocks that will take many years to smooth out. Post-1998, Benromach is essentially a new distillery and no attempt was made to copy the old whisky. Nonetheless, the present-day make has a similar character to the old, with cereal, malty tones, some citrus and spice, but also a touch of peat.

The first appearance of the new Benromach is in the Benromach Traditional (2004), which has no age statement and is lemony and floral (as you might expect a Forres whisky to be) with just a hint of spice and maltiness. This whisky is very affordable. Craig Moffat of Gleneagles Hotel has designed a cocktail with Benromach Traditional as its heart, called the Black Forres Gateaux (Mix 5cl Benromach Traditional, 2cl Chambord Royal Liqueur and a tea-spoonful of blackcurrant jam in a cocktail shaker with ice. Strain into a chilled Martini glass and float 1.5cl of double cream on top).

In 2006, Benromach produced an organic whisky, which may well be the first of its kind. Other Benromach expressions are inevitably older and therefore more expensive. There is always a premium to be paid for 'history in a glass'.

Keith Cruickshank kindly set up a vertical tasting for me. The hallmark seemed to be elegance and finesse; here are some of the impressions that stuck in my mind:

Benromach Traditional — very flowery, like a bouquet or a florist's shop. Also has puff candy, Liquorice Allsorts and spice. Refreshing and easy drinking.

Benromach 21 yr old — nose of lemon balm and deep floral notes. Lemon sponge cake, honey and spice on the palate. Clove rock in the aftertaste, warming the cockles of the heart.

Benromach 25 yr old — nose has plums, apricots and millionaire shortbread; more citric with water. Taste: a 'nippy sweetie' with rich marmalade and a numbing, nutmeg effect. My kind of dram!

Benromach 1980 cask strength — vanilla, tobacco and pure temptation in the nose. Sweet, fiery and substantial on the palate.

Benromach 22 yr old Portwood finish — nose has beer kegs and Battenberg cake. Taste is very fruity with a growing glow. Even the empty glass continues to give pleasure.

Benromach 1968 vintage — nose has apricots, sultanas and spice with a touch of smoke; reminiscent of armagnac. Lovely sherried flavour; dry, sweet and fruity.

SCOOBY THE CAT

One thing Gordon & MacPhail did inherit from United Distillers was Scooby, the distillery cat. Legend has it that Scooby was part of the deed of sale. Whether that is true or not, Gordon & MacPhail agreed to look after him, and look after him they did. During the refurbishment years, Scooby had an account at the Company's deli in Elgin and a member of staff came through every few days with the finest of food for him. He was undoubtedly the best-fed distillery cat in history.

He also had the run of the place and, as Keith Cruickshank recalls, 'He was the boss. He liked to sit in the middle of the manager's desk and no one dreamed of shifting him.' I asked if he had earned his keep; Keith said, 'Oh, no! He was a useless mouser. He was far too well fed. If the mouse had been cooked and served on a plate he might just consider eating it but that was about it. He was just a big fat cat.' The boss, indeed. Scooby died in 2000 and there has been no attempt to replace him.

LOVE IN THE MALT BARNS

(Tales from a Distillery)

One of the visitors to Benromach this September was a Jim Wylie from Invergowrie, near Dundee. During the winter of 1941, Jim, as a 19 year old piper in the Black Watch was billeted at Benromach. On Friday evenings he would play on the pipes at dances held in the Malt Barns. Sheena Begg, a local lass, fancied the young soldier. Love blossomed and the marriage, 57 years on, still flourishes. Mr Wylie remembers well the 'sodgers' washing in freezing cold water in the old Barley Steeps and making regular contributions to where the present tree nursery is. That's where the latrines were to be found and where, according to Jim and now confirmed by Bobby McCoach — our present gardener — you'll find the greenest grass in all of Forres.

From James Macpherson,
Special Projects Manager,
Gordon & MacPhail

DALLAS DHU

DALLAS DHU IS UNIQUE in Speyside, indeed in Scotland, for it is the only distillery that has been turned into a museum. Dallas Dhu is now managed by Historic Scotland and is undoubtedly in safe hands. Visitors can take the tour, just like in a working distillery, though nothing moves, everything is silent, there is no noise in the mill room and no heat comes from the stills. The workers one sees are models. Every part of the distillery seems intact, from the malt barns to the filling store, and in theory it could start production again — though I would say that is extremely unlikely. Sad as it might be to see Dallas Dhu forever silent, it is good to know that it will not be casually swept away, as many other former distilleries have been.

Dallas Dhu was the brainchild of Alexander Edwards. It was designed by Charles Doig, architect of 56 distilleries, and was the last distillery to be built in the 19th century (in 1899), born into the worst whisky recession in history. Edwards sold it on to the Glasgow based blenders Wright and Greig Ltd. Their best known brand was Roderick Dhu, which was selling very well in India and the Antipodes at that time. The original name for the distillery was to have been Dallasmore, but Wright and Greig changed it to Dallas Dhu. This means 'valley of the black water', but may well have been chosen for its resonance with the company's main blend.

Incidentally, the distillery lies a few miles from the tiny village of Dallas. The more famous city of the same name in Texas was named after a vice-president of the USA, George Dallas, a descendant of William de Ripley, who founded the Scottish village in 1297. Perhaps the two places should be twinned.

The history of Dallas Dhu is one of ups and downs as fortune dealt its capricious cards. The distillery was owned by Benmore Distillers from 1921. DCL took over Benmore in 1929 and immediately closed the place down. It remained mothballed until 1936, when it was reopened. On 9 April 1939, a fire destroyed the stillhouse, along with a considerable amount of other equipment. The damage was very quickly repaired and the distillery was back in production before the end of the year. Then war broke out and the Dallas whisky palace was shut down yet again.

After the war, the distillery enjoyed a few years of continuous working, investment and modernisation. However, in 1983, along with several other older, smaller distilleries in the group, it was finally closed. The last cask was filled on 16 March of that year. Dallas Dhu whisky can still be found, though it is becoming increasingly rare. If you visit the distillery you will not be offered a dram of Dallas Dhu, but rather the blend, Roderick Dhu.

DALLASMORE BENROMACH

Benromach and Dallas Dhu are appropriately remembered together in this poem, which I found in John Lamond's book, The Whisky Connoisseur's Companion. *He gives the author as 'J. McP. G.' and says it appeared in the* Forres Gazette *on 8 June 1898.*

Say you that the Forres trade is dull?
'Tis only just a little lull;
Just wait you till you fill your mull
With Dallasmore Benromach.

What, can't we sell our barley well?
Just wait again and you shall tell
What prices we so soon shall spell
With Dallasmore and Benromach.

The Guardian too, says we've no draff,
But here again we well can laugh.
Wait till the spirits pure you quaff
Of Dallasmore Benromach.

The whisky fever's touched us here,
And now we know there's naught to fear.
We'll make the rest look blooming queer
With Dallasmore Benromach.

Then out upon you poor Strathspey,
And all the rest Glenlivet way;
You'll find it mighty hard to pay
With Dallasmore Benromach.

GLENBURGIE

GLENBURGIE DISTILLERY IS SOMETHING of an enigma. When Barnard visited in 1886 he could describe it as 'a very ancient distillery, and about as old-fashioned as it is possible to conceive. It is said to be one of the oldest distilleries in the north.' Yet when I visited Glenburgie, 120 years later, it was undoubtedly the most modern distillery in the whole of Scotland. It is a fine example of how distilleries, like mayflies, can emerge shining and fresh from an old skin, once beautiful and useful but now discarded.

The origins of the distillery are slightly misted over by time. Barnard tells us that 'it was founded in the year 1810 by the grandfather of the celebrated surgeon, Dr Liston Paul, of London.' William Paul was indeed connected with a distillery at East Grange, near Forres, which was called the Grange Distillery and which may have been built in 1810. It seems he took it over from his father, John Paul, in 1826. The official records suggest that the present distillery commenced production in 1829. William Paul was the owner and the distillery was called Kilnflat (the name of the local farm). William ran the distillery until 1871, at which point it closed. Perhaps he retired or died; in any event the distillery lay silent until 1878, when it was resuscitated by Charles Kay and put back into production.

It was at this stage that it became known as Glenburgie, or Glenburgie-Glenlivet to be precise. From the comments Barnard made, it would seem that Kay did not undertake any great programme of modernisation upon reopening the distillery. Indeed, within four years or so it had passed into the ownership of Alexander Fraser, who was the proprietor at the time of Barnard's visit. In 1925 the company was bankrupted and control passed to a keen attorney from Elgin called Donald Mustard. He shut the place down and no doubt made a sharp deal when he sold it a few years later to George Ballantine and Sons, a subsidiary of Hiram Walker.

The most recent chapter of the distillery's history began when it went back into production in 1936, to make good quality malt to be used as the mainstay of Ballantine's blends. (That is still the case, though corporate ownership has changed through takeovers by Allied Distillers and, most recently, Pernod Ricard.) Glenburgie was fairly unusual in having a woman appointed as distillery manager.

Margaret Nicol managed the distillery for 24 years until she retired in 1959, so she must have done a reasonable job.

In 1958, Ballantine's installed two Lomond stills at Glenburgie. This was a time of experimentation and the idea behind the Lomond stills was to allow a distillery to produce several different types of spirit with the same equipment. This gives added flexibility in the production of blends. Lomond stills have a wider than usual, column-shaped neck with three rectifying plates inside, which can be adjusted in angle to create different degrees of reflux. Other adjustments are also possible. They were designed by Alistair Cunningham in 1955 and were installed at Glenburgie, Miltonduff and in the Inverleven part of the Dumbarton complex. They were removed from Glenburgie in 1981.

Today, there is a Lomond still (without the rectifying plates) working as a wash sill at Scapa distillery. Loch Lomond distillery has a Lomond-type still, though I do not think it is one of the originals, and the one from Dumbarton is hidden away in a quiet part of Islay, awaiting resurrection, though I can say no more as I am sworn to secrecy. The whisky made in the Lomond stills at Glenburgie was called Glencraig. It was said to be richer, heavier, more oily and more fruity than a Glenburgie, though Alex Kraaijeveld has challenged the frequently repeated statement that Lomond stills produce an oilier spirit. Glencraig was named after Willie Craig, production director at the time. His son, Bill, became general manager of Hiram Walker's Highland malt operations and another Willie Craig is now one of the operators at Glenburgie. The Craigs are therefore a bit of a Glenburgie dynasty, much like the Pauls were in the early days.

One building from the original distillery still stands in the grounds. It looks incongruous, surrounded by modern warehouses and the new distillery. In the early 19th century it contained offices and a tiny cellar for the maturation of casks. There are plans to turn the building into a Ballantine's Heritage Centre, which will probably not be open to the general public. In Barnard's day, the distillery produced 24,000 gallons a year (nearly 110,000 litres). In the late 1950s the floor maltings were removed and production was doubled by introducing two new stills. The present distillery has an annual capacity of 2.8 million litres with imminent plans to increase that to 4.2 million litres; a good example of how the scale of whisky production generally has expanded over the decades.

The present Glenburgie distillery was built from scratch on a site immediately adjacent to the old one. The former distillery was kept in production until the stills, the boiler and the mill were needed in their new home. At that point, production ceased for less than six months, until the transfer was organised and the finishing touches were incorporated. All traces of the old distillery were removed and the new plant went into action on 3 June 2005.

The new Glenburgie was designed by Ewan Fraser and its guiding principles were ease of operation and energy efficiency. The distillery has an open layout, mostly on one level, and can be controlled easily by the plant operator. The tallest part of the plant, containing the malt bins, is situated in the centre, with the mashing and distilling to one side and the fermentation to the other. Inside the distillery building there is a tremendous sense of open, airy space. Everything is gleaming; every tool has its designated space on the wall. All pipes and other potential trip and bump hazards are hidden away under the steel mesh floor. This is a clean and shiny new distillery. Every part of the process, apart from the cutting of the spirit run, is operated automatically. Glenburgie has been able to reduce its total staff complement from 10 to five, not including staff employed in the extensive warehousing on the site.

The energy efficiency measures are impressive. There is, for example, a heat recovery system on the wash stills. These have an external heater which reuses steam from the condensers, which would otherwise be lost, thanks to a thermal compressor. The underbelly of each still is coated in a thermal paint developed by NASA. Glenburgie has a similar output to Strathisla but uses only half the energy; they are very proud of their achievement of 20mJ a litre. This is one of the most important areas for achieving technological advances in distilling in the coming decades, given the inevitable increase in fuel costs.

The new distillery building at Glenburgie reemployed the stills from the old distillery. At first sight the four stills look very similar but on closer inspection it is clear they are subtly different. There is room on the floor to add a further pair of stills and that is exactly the plan. At the time of my visit, the extra space was occupied by a garden table, complete with impressive parasol, which seemed a bit odd, since the whole thing was indoors. In any case, I doubt there is much chance of loafing around, even in an automated distillery.

Water supply has always been a bit of an issue for Glenburgie and process water comes from a series of springs while the cooling water, which is dammed from a burn, is recycled back into the dam. In the future, there will be a water treatment plan installed and aquifer water will be accessed by boreholes.

The grist from the mill at Glenburgie is relatively fine; just enough to allow maximum extraction of sugars without clogging up the mash tun floor. It has four washes at the mashing stage to assist this. Fermentation used to be in a mixture of wooden and stainless steel washbacks but now all 12 are stainless steel. Glenburgie has a reasonably lengthy fermentation period, though this will change when the new stills are added. An unusually complex mixture of yeasts is used, including distillers' and brewers' yeasts, in fresh and dried form, from different suppliers.

All these things make a difference to the final spirit. Glenburgie new-make has traditionally had a nutty character but there is a chance that this will change with the new process. The fact that a malt whisky is nearly all lost in blends does not mean that it is of poor quality. Aeneas MacDonald, in his 1930s book *Whisky*, included Glenburgie as one of his 12 greatest malts. Glenburgie, and more rarely Glencraig, have been bottled from time to time by the 'independents', including Gordon & MacPhail and the Scotch Malt Whisky Society. The official bottling at 15 years old (46 per cent abv) has slate, pencil shavings, plum jam, orange peel and Ferrero Rocher chocolates on the nose and tastes warm and full-bodied, with flavours of jammy dodgers and hot spice. There is also a delicious 25 year old at full strength, which is sadly only available to company employees.

Glenburgie is the malt whisky most clearly associated with Ballantine's, which is the third biggest selling blended Scotch whisky in the world. A few years ago I bought a bottle of Ballantine's Finest at an airport in New York. After one taste I consigned it for use in the kitchen. Recently, just after Pernod Ricard took over Allied Distillers, I was in the company of Chivas' Douglas Callander one evening in Keith. He convinced me to try Ballantine's 17 year old. I found it such a delightful example of the blender's art that my prejudices fell away instantly. Then we finished the bottle and Douglas produced a bottle of Ballantine's Finest, just to see how far my prejudices (or my judgement) had subsided; he laughed at my reaction.

MONKY BUSINESS

The area around Glenburgie has an ancient link with distilling. Barnard described it as 'situated in the centre of the finest barley growing district of the north' and that is still true today. From the top of the malt bins you can see the huge maltings at Roseile and Burghead, up at the coast. This is a region where the spirit of John Barleycorn walks the land. Why else would the de Moravia family (who gave their name to Moray) have built their castle at nearby Duffus when they had the pick of the country following the Norman Conquest?

One of the distillery workers told me that there is a legend of an underground link between Glenburgie distillery and Kinloss Abbey. This has some credibility as monks were always at the forefront of developing alcoholic beverages.

Records in Keith show that one Thomas Crystal, 22nd Abbot at Kinloss, operated several 'brasinas' in the area.

The nearest village to Glenburgie is Alves, where, on Knock Hill, Macbeth is supposed to have met with the weird sisters who foretold his future, or at least that part of it in which he becomes king. It seems perfectly possible that Macbeth did not meet three witches with a cauldron at all, but rather three monks round a mashing vessel — and Macbeth, having sampled some of their aqua vitae, didn't remember things too well but felt that some kind of spell must have been involved. Thus, Shakespeare, unwittingly, may have given us one of the first historical accounts of whisky-making in Scotland.

INCHGOWER

INCHGOWER DISTILLERY WAS BUILT in 1871 by Alexander Wilson. It was a replacement for the abandoned distillery of Tochineal, some 10 miles to the west near Cullen. The Countess of Seafield apparently did not like having a distillery on her land so she and the Earl doubled the rent, driving the enterprise away from Tochineal. The Wilson family made the best of the situation and Inchgower was constructed as a model distillery which very quickly built a fine reputation.

Barnard made his visit here 'on a bright summer morning with an Italian sky over our heads.' He travelled by carriage from Fochabers station and describes with great appreciation the landscape encountered in crossing the Spey, the policies of Gordon Castle and the hilly landscapes from Ben Aigen and Ben Rinnes to 'the famous Bin Hill of Cullen ...standing out in bold relief from

a background of blue sky.' He found himself 'in the midst of scenes which no pen could justly describe or pencil delineate', but that did not stop him from trying.

He was particularly taken with the 'glorious and expansive view of the sea and the hills of Sutherlandshire across the Moray Firth' and with the agricultural bounties of 'this rich and fertile country.' He goes on, 'We passed broad acres of goldening grain, studded over with gaudy cornflowers and ornamented with lines of beautiful trees. Here and there were patches of wild flowers, growing in the rose-covered hedges.' The environment is still eye-catchingly attractive and, as I was leaving Inchgower, it was not an oyster catcher (the bird on the flora and fauna bottle) but a heron that flapped a farewell over straw bales and stubble fields.

The area was then, and continues to be, one of the more fertile parts of the Laigh of Moray. Barnard tells us the distillery was attached to 'a farm of 200 acres, and a model farm-steading arranged on new sanitary principles. Upwards of 100 head of black-polled cattle, nearly 200 sheep, and a quantity of pigs, all bred on the farm, are fed the burnt ale and draff, conveyed by gravitation from the Distillery to the farm buildings.' There is something idyllic about this picture Barnard paints of the symbiotic relationship between distilling and agriculture. That relationship continues to exist but not now on such a micro-local basis.

Barnard described a distillery 'of handsome elevation and the buildings, which are of stone, and slated, are erected in the form of an oblong quadrangle.' Around this quadrangle were the maltings, the engine house, warehouses, offices, a cooperage and carpenter's shop, a smithy and 'a noble building' containing mash house, tun room and still-house. This still-house he describes as having 'a lofty and church-like appearance... lighted by stained windows, quite a suitable habitation for the perfection of barley into a perfect spirit.' In front of the two stills was 'space sufficient to seat a small congregation of spectators to witness the progress of the work and spiritual mission carried on within its boundaries.'

Many of these functions have disappeared over the years, along with the farm and the stained windows, but the layout of the distillery quadrangle and the workers' cottages is still pretty much the way it was in the 1880s. In 1966 the maltings were removed and the stills doubled to four. In 1885 there were six washbacks, as now, but in those days they were made on-site by

the distillery carpenters and the total capacity was 86,000 litres, whereas now it is 240,000 litres. The annual output has soared from about 280,000 litres to around 2.3 million litres. Once again we see that wonderful balance between tradition and innovation, between continuity and dynamic change, that is the history and the reality of whisky-making.

The distillery is less than two kilometres from the seashore and on the eastern and southern side is a long vista of hills, including the remarkable Bin of Cullen to the east, and its flanking neighbours Little Bin and Hill of Maud, which make up an Eildon-like trilogy. Further off to the south are the various hills of the forested Aultmore, which Barnard has as the setting for a smuggler story. It is from these hills that the Inchgower water source comes. Barnard mentions the Letter Burn, which flows from the Hill of Menduff and provides the distillery's process water. Cooling water comes from the Burn of Buckie.

Inchgower is the most coastal of the Speyside malts and, since it seems that, until fairly recently at least, the casks put aside for bottling as single malt were matured on-site, there is a chance that some of its flavour profile may reflect its coastal position. Many people, including the current owners Diageo, deny that such factors make any significant difference.

Barnard was treated to dinner at the Arradoul residence of Alexander Wilson and it is hard to imagine that they did not share a dram of Inchgower. However, all he says is that 'it is considered clean and mellow to the palate and much appreciated by connoisseurs.' I used to drink a fair amount of Inchgower in the 1970s, when it had 'Bell's Inchgower' on the bottle, though in recent years I have had very little experience of it. So perhaps Michael Jackson should have the last word: 'To the palate expecting a more flowery, elegant Speyside style, this can seem assertive, or even astringent in its saltiness. With familiarity, that can become addictive.'

TOCHINEAL

The distillery of Tochineal was opened in 1825 and closed in 1867. It had established a strong reputation and when it was resurrected in 1871 the workers were all given the chance to move. Many did, but not all. There was obviously sadness about leaving the old distillery and perhaps some resentment over the reasons for the move.

In the Inchgower still-house visited by Barnard, 'Against the wall, at the end of the building, there is placed a grandfather's clock, a relic of the old Tochineal Distillery, which keeps time better than any other clock on the premises.' He also commented on the workers; 'We noticed that most of the workmen were middle-aged or elderly, and of a superior class, and were informed that most of them came from the Old Distillery, and had been with the firm all their lives.' Traces of Tochineal distillery can still be seen at Lintmill near Cullen and the feelings and views of the workers have come down to us in the classic form of the North East of Scotland — the folk song:

Come a' my young lads, ye'll mak haste and
    be ready,
For May twenty-saxt will be here in a crack,
An we ane an a', but the man in the smiddy,
Maun leave Tochineal, nae mair to come back.

Awa to the West we maun a' gang thegither,
The men, wives and wee anes, wi' true herts
    and leal,

An our wives they will a' be in a sad swither,
On that awfu' day that we leave Tochineal.

Aucht wives in a hoose wi' a brick separation,
I niver ance thocht it wad dee very weel,
For their tongues were sae rid for tae
    gie provocation,
There could be nae contentment at auld
    Tochineal.

There were Jamie and Sandy, and Archie
    and Watty,
There were Walker and Taylor, and Forbes
    and Kemp,
We were aucht jolly lads, but we're jist
    something chatty,
When ance we get in the wee drappie o' drink.

We're aul', and we're wracket, to work we'd
    nae scruple,
Our joints they are stiff and that we do feel,
They're no like our wives' tongues, for faith
    they're richt supple,
When they think we've been drinking the
    pure Tochieneal.

But what is a' this but a blether o' nonsense,
There's nane o's been there yet that grievance
    to feel,
But there's ae thing I'll say, without hurting
    my conscience,
The bye-word will be this is nae Tochieneal.

ELGIN

Elgin, the capital town of Moray, lies on the River Lossie.
It was made a Royal Burgh in the 13th century; the original
Elgin Cathedral also dates from this time. Part of the town and the
cathedral were burned to the ground in 1390 by the Wolf of Badenoch.
Elgin retains some traces of its medieval past, as well as being the
administrative centre of the area and a hub of the whisky business.

**BENRIACH
GLEN ELGIN
GLEN MORAY
GLENLOSSIE
GORDON & MACPHAIL
LINKWOOD
LONGMORN
MANNOCHMORE
MILTONDUFF**

Photo: Robin Laing

BENRIACH

UNLOCK THE SECRETS

BENRIACH IS ANOTHER OF those distilleries born in the boom of the late 1890s, coming into production in 1898. It was commissioned by John Duff, who had built Longmorn four years previously. Indeed, Benriach (meaning either 'Hill of the Red Deer' or 'Speckled Mountain', depending on who you ask) was built on a site adjacent to Longmorn and was sometimes known as Longmorn No 2. It was designed by Charles Doig of Elgin. Following the Pattison's crash, it closed down in 1900 and remained silent for 65 years. In 1965, at another time of growth in the whisky industry, it was completely refurbished and revitalised.

During most of the silent years, the maltings continued to operate, providing malt for other distilleries. Benriach was bought over by Seagrams in 1978, eventually becoming part of the Chivas group (now owned by Pernod Ricard). The whole distillery ceased production again in 1999. In 2004, it was sold to the Benriach Distillery Company Ltd, headed by Billy Walker, previously managing director of Burn Stewart. Under the new ownership, the distillery and its single malt expressions are experiencing something of a revival.

The maltings have been beautifully maintained and look ready to spring back into action — there was even a laid fire of sticks sitting in the kiln furnace when I was shown round by Alan MacConnachie. MacConnachie is the distillery manager, and came to Benriach from Tobermory distillery. The Benriach Distillery Company apparently intends a phased recommissioning of the maltings. This is an interesting development that represents a reversal of an industry trend over the last few decades, which has been to take grain management and malting off-site. At least one other distillery is planning a similar move and the motivation seems to be only partly to do with presenting an attractive heritage experience to visitors.

The Porteus Mill at Benriach is slightly unusual. It dates from 1965, when it was specially made for an exposition, and is enamelled inside. Perhaps because of this, it is protected by two de-stoners. The mash tun is stainless steel, but with traditional rake and arm gear inside. Also of stainless steel are the eight washbacks, which provide normal fermentation of at least 48 hours, though this stretches to between 65 and 100 hours at weekends. The number of stills, of traditional onion shape, was increased from two to four in 1985.

When the distillery was acquired from Pernod Ricard in 2004, it came with significant stocks of whisky. Benriach has five dunnage warehouses on-site, with a storage capacity of 30,000 casks. This has allowed the new owners to issue an interesting portfolio of single malts, which includes the no-age-statement Heart of Speyside, the 12, 16 and 20 year olds, and occasional other vintages and finishes. Benriach used to be mainly directed into blends and was rare as a single malt. Now that is likely to change; the main thrust will be to market a single malt brand. Independent bottlings are reasonably easy to find and there is still some of the 10 year old proprietary bottling produced by Chivas, but that is becoming rare.

The biggest secrets to be unlocked at Benriach are undoubtedly the peated versions. Chivas had been experimenting with peated malt at Benriach and at Caperdonich, though they released none of the whisky as single malts. The new owners were quick to release, first, a 10 year old peated malt under the name of Curiositas, followed by a 21 year old called Authenticas. In the days of Alfred Barnard a Speyside whisky that was not peated would have been considered a

curiosity. Some stock of peated whisky from first fill sherry casks exists, which should be interesting, but has not yet been released. Benriach currently uses both unpeated and peated (at 35ppm) barley, for two separate spirit productions.

Benriach does not have a visitor centre in the conventional sense. Billy Walker says that the whole distillery is a visitor centre and that the aim is to provide personalised tours. Obviously, advance booking is advisable, though as far as possible, they will not turn people away. A cottage on-site, previously the manager's home, has been turned into an attractive, small-scale, wood-panelled facility for entertaining guests and conducting tastings.

Also in the cottage is the sample room. Alan MacConnachie offered me a taste of various samples of both peated and unpeated vintages. The 1966, which is the oldest stock still available at Benriach, was gorgeously deep and plumy, and the peated samples from 1986 and 1994 are characterised by a stiff and unmistakable smoke, but with fruit and spice rather than the

iodine and antiseptic that we have come to expect from some of the island malts.

From the twinkling lights of endless rows of sample bottles containing all the varied yellow, gold and orange hues of matured whisky, I stepped out into fresh air and an evening sun shining on cottages and harvested fields. The landscape was bright and lively, like a Jolomo painting. As I left Benriach behind, the sun was fading and I saw the tall white windmills over on Cairn Uish slowly turning and reflecting the last of the bright light like revolving beacons. Such is the power whisky has to make the world shine in bright sharp focus — just before the lights go out.

Another Benriach moment occurred a few months later at the Craigellachie Hotel. I was sitting outside in the spring sunshine with Soren and Birthe Gabriel, the hotel owners at that time, planning the evening event for the Spirit of Speyside Whisky Festival. The hotel's quaich bar has perhaps the most impressive whisky selection in Scotland. It also has a special locked cabinet for members of the Craigellachie Club. Members (and there is a waiting list) keep their special whisky in that cabinet for their own private access. It is very interesting to have a peek and see who has what as their special bottle.

The Gabriels offered me a dram from theirs; a 29 year old Benriach. Looking out over the Spey and Telford Bridge in good company was the perfect setting for such a quintessentially Speyside dram. The sun shone beautifully, birds twittered wantonly and it seemed we were witnessing the very bud-burst of Spring. The Benriach, with its exotic fruits and coconut, went to my head and to my soul at the same time, as any really good whisky should.

WILLIE BREW'D A PECK O MAUT (Extract)

Robert Burns

We are na fou, we're nae that fou,
But just a drappie in oor e'e!
The cock may craw, the day may daw',
But aye we'll taste the barley bree.

GLEN ELGIN

GLEN ELGIN IS ONE of a necklace of distilleries on the road between Elgin and Rothes. Incidentally, there is no such glen; the name was simply made up at a time when Elgin was growing in stature as a regional whisky centre. It lies next to the Millbuies country park, in a very charming setting.

Few distilleries highlight the disastrous days that beset the whisky industry at the birth of the 20th century better than Glen Elgin. It was established in 1898 and construction began in the same year. However, the construction was delayed; it is said, because of a shortage of capital. That might seem strange as one of the founders, James Carle, was a banker (the other was William Simpson, who had previously managed Glenfarclas). Perhaps bankers are more familiar with the forced closure and sale of distilleries than with their creation.

Distillation eventually started at the beginning of May 1900 and the final cost of the distillery, designed by Charles Doig, was over £13,000. Then the balloon of optimism which had seen such a wave of new distilleries, especially in Speyside, was rudely punctured by the Pattison's scandal and the foul air that came out caused many a distiller to choke. Glen Elgin ceased production only five or six months after it had started. In February 1901 it was put up for auction, but was withdrawn as bids did not reach

the reserve price of £5,000. On 25 July it was auctioned again (one can sense the growing desperation) and was sold to an anonymous bidder for £4,000.

After being bought by Scottish Malt Distillers in 1930, it became the mainstay malt in the famous White Horse blend. In the 1950s, the entire distillery was still

powered by paraffin and water power but a lot of whisky has passed through the Glen Elgin worms since then. It was expanded and practically rebuilt in 1964, when the number of stills rose from two to six. These stills, although conventional in shape, have quite a flat, pancake flare profile between neck and body.

Glen Elgin has long been valued by blenders, but not often encountered as a single malt, apart from a number of independent bottlings and under the proprietary Flora and Fauna range (with a picture of a house martin). All that is likely to change soon as it is one of the single malts that has been chosen by Diageo for a marketing boost, following on from the success of the Classic Malts (the others include Caol Ila, Gen Ord, Dufftown and Clynelish). As a result of this, there has been some recent investment in the plant, including the installation of a Steineker full-lauter mash tun.

Glen Elgin has had its ups and downs but it is essentially a survivor. Despite its inauspicious start and the usual hiccups along the way, the future is now looking bright for this distillery and its excellent product.

WHISKY JOHNNY

Oh whisky is the life of man
Whisky Johnny!
Whisky from an old tin can
Whisky for me Johnny!

Whisky made me sell my coat
Whisky Johnny!
Whisky's what keeps me afloat
Whisky for me Johnny!

Whisky gave me many a sigh
Whisky Johnny!
But I'll swig whisky till I die
Whisky for me Johnny!

Whisky killed me poor ol' Dad
Whisky Johnny!
Whisky druv me mother mad
Whisky for me Johnny!

Whisky made me pawn me cloes
Whisky Johnny!
Whisky gave me this red nose
Whisky for me Johnny!

Whisky up and whisky down
Whisky Johnny!
Oooh! Whisky all around the town
Whisky for me Johnny!

GLEN MORAY

GLEN MORAY DISTILLERY CAME to life in 1897, when Henry Arnott's West Brewery was converted to a distillery by Robert Thorne and Sons of Greenock, owners of Aberlour distillery. At the time of Barnard's visit, this would still have been a brewery and therefore not worthy of his attention, as it only took the nectar-making process halfway. It was first established as the Glen Moray Glenlivet Distillery Company — one of the furthest of all the 'Glenlivets' from the stream of that name.

Actually, Glen Moray is a Lossie whisky; the distillery site, on the outskirts of Elgin, is practically surrounded by the River Lossie and that location makes it vulnerable to flooding. A flood level plaque on the side of one of the buildings shows the height of record flooding in November 2002. A recent flood, which saw the water level rise to four feet, affected all the warehouses, and some casks died. Whatever your position on the 'water with whisky' debate, this would not be desirable.

Glen Moray has a massive 1,200 tonnes capacity for malt storage in its 18 malt bins. At one time, the distillery had Saladin Box maltings, though that was stopped in the 1980s, and the generous holding capacity no doubt relates to those days. Nonetheless, the ability to store considerable amounts of malt means that Glen Moray can buy in bulk when prices are good. This can make a difference, considering that malt represents about 50 per cent of the costs of a distillery operation. Glen Moray does not favour any particular type of barley, so the strain changes from time to time. While having an obvious financial advantage, this means that they must be very careful to check the grind regularly. Malted barley can vary considerably from one batch to another and fine adjustments to the rollers in the mill can be necessary to get the appropriate make-up of the grist.

Fortunately, the malt storage is well above the level of the occasional floods. Indeed, the malt storage building is so high that the view from the top extends over all the wide, pleasant lands of the Laigh of Moray and across the town of Elgin. From up there, one is also astonished by the extent of the warehousing below, which consists of eight dunnage and two palletised warehouses, within which 50,000 casks lie breathing imperceptibly in the dim light.

Five stainless steel washbacks represent just a bit of a bottle neck in the production process and, perhaps for that reason, fermentation is fairly brisk at 40 hours or so.

The number of stills was increased from two to four in 1958. One still has recently had a new neck fitted, which, I was informed, cost around £1,200. These are expensive kettles!

Graham Coull, the distillery manager, showed me around. Graham had recently moved to Glen Moray from William Grant & Sons to replace the long-serving Edwin Dodson on his retirement. My visit to warehouse number one was a particular treat. There, I saw some big sherry wood — fat gordas and bodega butts. I also saw the casks that had been filled for the Scotch Malt Whisky Society; four gordas (1996) and 12 first fill bourbon barrels (1998). I shall look forward to those coming

through the tasting panel. There were plenty of Glen Moray's own interesting casks in there too and, when we got back to the visitor centre, I was able to try a few, with Graham on hand to explain the pedigree of each dram.

Glen Moray used to produce a series of attractive tins decorated with the livery of various Highland regiments, which are now collectables. The present Glen Moray portfolio of single malts consists of the Classic (no age statement but about 8 years old), the 12 year old and the 16 year old. The range of white wine finishes (pioneered by Glen Moray and including whiskies mellowed in Chardonnay and Chenin Blanc wine casks) can still be found but seems to have been discontinued. I was very fond of the Chardonnay finished Glen Moray so I was sad to hear that it is no more.

However, experimentation still goes on, as you might expect from a distillery that is owned by Glenmorangie. I was privileged to sample a Centenary Port Finish dram and to try some of their Mountain Oak single cask malts. These are full strength (60.2 per cent abv) whiskies matured in virgin oak (some charred and some toasted); very bourbon-like, but beautiful. Finally, a taste of the 42 year old (1962) vintage had me dumbstruck with reverence for its deep character of bountiful Christmas joy.

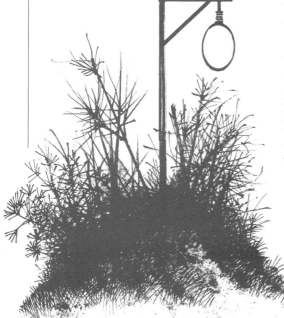

SKULL-DUGGERY

One of the blends that Glen Moray contributes to is the Baillie Nichol Jarvie. That whisky is named after a character from Scott's Rob Roy who had to fight off a drunken Highlander with a firebrand. To commemorate that event, there is today a poker hanging from a tree in the village of Aberfoyle. Darker things have hung from trees in Elgin.

Elgin was (and is) the capital town of Moray and many criminals were tried, convicted and punished there over the centuries. For a long time, the place of execution was on Gallows Crook Hill, which happens to be very close to warehouse number one at Glen Moray distillery. In the bad old days, murderers, thieves and witches were 'brint to the death, hanged by the craig, or droont'. Those who were hanged were left hanging in chains as grisly reminders to the populace of the fate awaiting evil-doers.

This still happened as late as 1810, when Alexander Gillan was hanged for ravishing and murdering Elizabeth Lamb. He was executed in public by a seemingly unskilled hangman whose 'whole concern seemed directed to the perquisites of the office more than the business in which he was engaged'.

'Having hung an hour, he was cut down and put into irons, and he now remains suspended from his gibbet, a shocking example of the dreadful effects of vice, when permitted to usurp the empire of reason; an example which, it is hoped, will strike deep into the minds of the rising generation, and tend to prevent the recurrence of such terrifying spectacles.'

Perhaps it was the same hangman who was set upon and chased out of Elgin by a crowd in 1834, immediately after the last execution in Moray. He crossed the Lossie at a place still known as Hangman's Ford and was later found dead from his injuries in Forres. The remains of the town gibbet were still visible into the 20th century.

In the 1960s, Glen Moray raised the floor of warehouse number one by spreading infill material taken from the hill above. This was to prevent the worst effects of flooding, to which that warehouse was particularly vulnerable. In excavating material from the hill, workmen discovered seven human skulls. One of the skulls was found to have a bullet-hole in its back and a lead ball embedded in the jaw. Whatever the story behind these skulls, they were reburied once the work was completed, but for a few weeks they were a grisly ornament in the still room. There is even an unverified story that one of them was taken for a drive around the town so he could see how things had changed in Elgin over the years.

When I visited Glen Moray, I was surprised to see some stocks (I don't mean whisky stocks) in a corridor. Were medieval punishments still being carried out in Elgin? Apparently these were just props from a fete, which had been temporarily stored in the distillery, but I moved quickly on in case they were reserved for visitors who asked too many questions.

GLENLOSSIE

GLENLOSSIE DISTILLERY IS SITUATED at Birnie, about four kilometres south of Elgin and one kilometre east of the River Lossie. Birnie seems to be a very historical site. There is considerable evidence of iron age fort settlements nearby and within the last 10 years a significant hoard of several hundred Roman coins was uncovered near the distillery. These date from just before 200 AD, the time of Emperor Severus, who ordered the last invasion of Scotland. A monument to Severus in York shows him wearing tartan trousers, which inevitably leads to speculation that his invasion was all about acquiring some Scottish cloth and whisky. Tourists have changed very little, really.

Also at Birnie is the famous Birnie Kirk. Built in 1140, this is one of the oldest churches in Scotland. In its early existence, it was the first cathedral of the Bishopric of Moray, until Elgin Cathedral was built in the 1200s. Even earlier, the site was a Celtic church dedicated to St Brendan the Navigator, the real discoverer of America. The church is beautiful and peaceful and contains a number of interesting artefacts, including the square Coronach Bell, which is said to be over 1,000 years old and to have been blessed by the Pope. The kirk also keeps the curious Hairy Bible, dated 1773, whose binding is of calfskin with the hair still attached.

At the time when Alfred Barnard visited 'Glen Lossie', the owner was a man called John Duff. It is a shame that Barnard had no meeting with Mr Duff, for he seems to have been quite a character.

Back in the 1870s, John Duff was the manager at Glendronach distillery and also ran an inn at Lhanbryde, just east of Elgin. Duff got together with two friends, Alexander Grigor Allen and H.M.S. MacKay (one was the local public prosecutor and the other the burgh surveyor) to build a new distillery. They brought in John Hopkins, whisky merchant, as a partner in the firm, and they leased the land from Lord Seafield. Barnard says the distillery was 'built by and under the supervision of Mr Duff, from his own plans'.

That was in 1876, and by 1888, shortly after Barnard's visit, Duff apparently became restless and saw an opportunity to spread the wonders of distilling to the New World. He took his family to the Transvaal and later to America, in the hope of setting up distilleries in those places. It appears that he lost a lot of money in the

Transvaal when his project was spoiled by President Kruger, who did not like British investors moving in. Duff returned to Scotland in 1892. In the mid 1890s, Duff's involvement with Glenlossie ended and he set up Longmorn distillery a short distance away. Then, in 1898, he established Benriach distillery, but by 1909 he was bankrupt, a victim of the fallout from the Pattison's crash.

It is fascinating to compare Barnard's account with today's situation at Glenlossie. In Barnard's day, the distillery was owned by John Duff, a real Victorian entrepreneur and daring adventurer, one of the great individuals of the whisky industry, almost single-handedly responsible for setting up three distilleries in the area. Now, Glenlossie is owned by the biggest multinational drinks company in the world — a corporate giant, which owns one-third of all the distilleries in Speyside.

Barnard describes how the work of the distillery is 'carried on entirely by water power and gravitation' and says the reservoir 'is supplied with water from the Mannoch Hills. There is also the Creich Spring in the hill, a quarter of a mile distant.' He then tells us that the kiln is 'heated with peat brought from the Mannoch Hills, five miles distant.' These days no peat is dug locally and very little is used in the malting process anyway, and water stopped providing the power long ago. However, cooling water still comes from the Mannoch Hills and the reservoir is still there. Strangely, in recent years a wind farm has been built on Cairn Uish and so once again it can be claimed that some of the power for the distillery comes from the Mannoch Hills.

Barnard talks about 'two handsome Old Pot Stills, both heated by furnaces.' Heating these days is by steam produced from an oil-fired boiler, but apart from that I understand that the size and shape of the stills is pretty much the same as it was in the 19th century. Glenlossie is one of the few distilleries to have purifiers on the spirit stills; they sit up on the back wall near the condensers. Unfortunately, Barnard did not mention these, so we do not know if they are a more recent addition. He did notice purifiers at Glen Grant, so it may be those at Glenlossie did not exist at the time. These days there are six stills at Glenlossie. Two were added in 1896 and another two in 1962. They are still undoubtedly 'handsome' and highly polished and sit in a gleaming and bright still-house.

The still-house in 1885 was the only part of the distillery that was stone-built; all the rest was made of a new-fangled material called concrete. Barnard says the distillery was 'constructed entirely of cement, which, under the sunlight, as we descended the hill, looked beautifully white and clean.' Remarkably, Glenlossie is still an attractive distillery, but Barnard would probably not recognise it. Output then was about 400,000 litres, whereas now potential capacity is 2.2 million. Also, Mannochmore has sprung up next door; the warehousing that is shared by the two distilleries has the capacity for 200,000 casks, compared with the 4,000 that could be stored in Barnard's day.

When John Duff was in charge, the operation included a farm with '50 head of cattle which are fattened on the draff and spent-wash of the distillery.' Such a cosy and agrarian arrangement no longer exists but the principle behind it still applies, though on a much larger scale. Around 1970, United Distillers took the forward-thinking step of building a huge dark grains plant here, involving around £7.4m investment. This plant was designed to handle the waste from eleven local distilleries, including some of UD's competitors. The scale of the plant is considerable; it can process 2,600 tonnes of draff and eight million litres of pot ale in a week, producing 1,000 tonnes of animal feed pellets.

Some things change in the detail but not in the underlying reality. Barnard, as usual, does not mention whether he tasted the whisky or how good it was. These days it is similarly hard to get hold of. Diageo produce a few bottles of the usual Flora and Fauna range and there are one or two independent bottlings; that's about it. Glenlossie is very popular with the blenders, considered 'top class' by many of them, and that's where it all goes, finding its way into a number of blends — traditionally it is one of the main components in Haig's.

UISGE BEATHA – PERFECTIO

BRACAE
TARTANRY
BREEKUS

TAM O' SHANTER (Extract)

Robert Burns

Inspiring bold John Barleycorn
What dangers thou canst make us scorn!
Wi tippenny, we fear nae evil;
Wi usquabae, we'll face the Devil!

GORDON & MACPHAIL

THE FIRM OF GORDON & MACPHAIL describes itself as 'the world's leading malt whisky specialist'. This is not an unreasonable claim. It is undoubtedly the longest standing and biggest of the independent bottlers of single malts, and at a time when it is increasingly difficult for independent bottlers to access good quality casks, Gordon & MacPhail's good reputation and solid and extensive network of business connections will stand them in good stead.

James Gordon and John Alexander MacPhail established their grocers and spirit merchants business in Elgin in May 1895. Speyside was, by that time, in the ascendant as a centre of distilling excellence, Elgin was fast becoming a hub of the whisky world and Scotch whisky was on a definite course for world domination. It was natural, therefore, that Gordon & MacPhail should see whisky as a central part of their enterprise.

Within a few months of the business's opening, John Urquhart, aged 15, started work as an apprentice. An able lad, he soon had considerable responsibility within the whisky side of the business. In 1915, John Alexander MacPhail retired and Urquhart became a partner in the firm. Two weeks later, James Gordon died suddenly and Urquhart was the senior partner and found himself running the show. It was a classic rags to riches story.

It was also the start of a whisky dynasty. His son, George, joined the firm in 1933 and made a real impact on the whisky landscape. He has been described as 'the saviour of single malts'. At a time when the only whisky language was 'blends', George, with great vision and some courage, continued to have belief in the value of the single malt. By World War II, Gordon & MacPhail had the largest selection of single malts in the world.

The company is now in the hands of the children and grandchildren of George Urquhart. Their holding of malt whisky is hugely impressive. They have casks from 87 distilleries in their Elgin warehouses and carry stocks of 460 own-bottled whiskies and more than 700 whiskies altogether. Between six and seven thousand casks are maturing in the company's new premises in George House, Elgin and they own about the same number again scattered around the country within distilleries. Some of their casks are more than 50 years old, with the oldest being a 1938 Mortlach in a sherry cask. Finally, they now also have their own distillery at Benromach, which represents the realisation of an ambition long cherished by George Urquhart.

When I visited the Gordon & MacPhail premises, I found the directors and the staff to be very hospitable and helpful. When they showed me the Aladdin's Cave of the warehouse I could not stop my eyes from popping and perhaps because of that they sat me down to sample a few of their products from the Rare Old, Cask Strength and Connoisseur's Choice ranges, while they told me about their impressive quality control policy. I remember a delightful 1975 St Magdalene, an inspirational 1964 Strathisla and a fantastic 1954 Linkwood, which had raisin and leafy bonfire aromas.

Oh, and they also still have the shop in South Street, Elgin, where there is an impressive selection of wines and foods and a great deli counter, as well as the famous whisky department.

TO CHARLES BAXTER (Extract)

Robert Louis Stevenson

But, freend, ye ken how me an' you,
The ling-lang lanely winter through,
Keep'd a guid speerit up an' true
To lore Horatian,
We aye the ither bottle drew —
To inclination.

Sae let us in the comin' days
Stand sicker on oor auncient ways —
The strauchest road in a' the maze
Since Eve ate apples;
An' let the winter weet oor cla'es —
We'll weet oor thrapples.

LINKWOOD

LINKWOOD IS ANOTHER TOP class malt in great demand by blenders. It has featured in White Horse, Haig, Bell's and Dimple. It is considered to be a light, sweet, fruity and complex whisky but in my experience, at full strength it can also be a bit of a bruiser. Some of the headlines for tasting notes I have written include 'Huge and Seemingly Indestructible', 'Explosive!', 'Coal Tar and Rose Petals' and 'Deep-Impact Dram'. This is no fainting damsel or pale-visaged milksop but a whisky with something to say for itself. It is not all that easy to come by and if I were the kind of person who considered collecting the whisky from one distillery, this might be a good choice.

Barnard had little to say about it. He drove out from Elgin (which he found 'an agreeable place') 'along a pleasant country road, amid smiling hedgerows and hayfields.' The distillery was 'embosomed in woods, hence its name.' Linkwood still lies just beyond the edge of Elgin, between the wonderfully named farms of Dunkinty and Barmuckity. The distillery, which lies very close to the Inverness to Aberdeen railway, is extremely attractive, with its woods and holding pond. If ever there was a whisky that deserves to be associated with Flora and Fauna it is Linkwood. The pond is visited or frequented by a dazzling variety of birdlife, including the mute swans which feature on the label. Otters have also been seen here and the surroundings are alive with butterflies and bees.

The grounds have been carefully tended for decades. This was the nearest distillery to the Elgin offices of United Distillers and so was kept in presentable condition for various VIP guests. *Whisky Magazine*, not long ago, recorded an interview with Hilary Lamont, the distillery gardener. Hilary had worked at Linkwood, tending the 10 acre grounds, for 25 years. At the time of the interview she was the only full time distillery gardener in

Scotland. She has now retired and the grounds will no doubt be looked after differently. Her work was responsible for the richness of plant cover and wildlife — over 530 species of animals, insects and birds had been counted at Linkwood.

The distillery was born in 1824, when Peter Brown started making whisky here. When he died, his son William took over. William was the proprietor at the time of Barnard's visit and Barnard tells us that he had rebuilt the distillery in 1873. The following year, the *Elgin Courant* reported that Linkwood had installed speaking tubes so that the miller, who had to be incarcerated in the mill room by order of the Customs and Excise, could communicate with the outside world if any emergency should occur.

The distillery passed into the hands of Scottish Malt Distillers Ltd in 1933. After the Second World War, a manager called Roderick Mackenzie from Wester Ross ruled over the place for 18 years. Poor Roderick may have been a touch superstitious and obsessive for he has passed into legend as the man who strove to avoid any change that might impact adversely on the whisky quality, even issuing an edict not to remove cobwebs in the still-house.

Such a living death was never going to be the fate for a distillery like Linkwood and sure enough in 1962 it was completely refurbished. Roderick appears to have left the company, or died of shock, within a few months of this. Then, in 1971, it was expanded by the construction next door of a second distillery with four stills. The new distillery takes care of the mashing but some of the wort is sent next door for fermentation and some of the wash continues to be distilled in the two old stills which, incidentally, retain their worm tubs.

Linkwood is thus a distillery where the Victorian and the modern sit side by side and work in harness together to produce upward of 2.5 million litres a year, about one or two per cent of which ends up as single malt.

SCOTCH DRINK (Extract)

Robert Burns

Let other poets raise a fracas
Bout vines an wines, an drunken Bacchus,
An crabbit names an stories wrack us,
An grate our lug:
I sing the juice Scotch bear can mak us,
In glass or jug.

Oh thou, my Muse! Guid auld Scotch drink!
Whether thro wimplin worms thou jink,
Or, richly brown, ream owre the brink,
In glorious faem,
Inspire me, till I lisp an wink,
To sing thy name.

Let husky wheat the haughs adorn,
An oats set up their awnie horn,
An pease and beans at e'en or morn,
Perfume the plain:
Leeze me on thee, John Barleycorn,
Thou king o' grain.

LONGMORN

SOMETHING SPECIAL

LONGMORN DISTILLERY WAS BUILT IN 1894, a couple of miles from Elgin. It stands next door to its sister distillery, Benriach, on the road south towards Rothes. The site, near a farm, was chosen for its water supply and for its proximity to the railway line that used to join Rothes to Elgin. The first train to make the journey set off on 1 January 1862. The public was able to buy a return ticket on that maiden run for the price of a single fare. During the distillery building boom of the 1890s, positioning near a railway made perfect sense. The old railway station can still be seen in the Longmorn distillery grounds. At one time, Longmorn had a distillery puggie for hauling freight between Longmorn and Benriach, and may have been connected to the main line.

The distillery was founded in 1893 by the same John Duff who established Glenlossie. In 1897, building on the great success of Longmorn, he established Benriach next door and bought out his two partners, George Thomson and Charles Shirres. Unfortunately, following the Pattison's crash, Duff found himself in serious debt and had to sell everything he owned, including Longmorn and its stock. He never really recovered from this and was eventually bankrupted in 1909. The Longmorn-Glenlivet Distillery Company Ltd continued to trade, under different ownership, until 1970, when it joined forces with Glen Grant and Glenlivet to become Glenlivet Distilleries Ltd. In 1978 it came under the ownership of Seagrams, and then in 2001 it passed to the present owners, Pernod Ricard.

The name Longmorn comes from early Gaelic and the meaning is a bit obscure. It is usually translated as 'The Place of the Holy Man', perhaps because the exact name of the holy man in question is unclear. St Morgund, St Morgan, St Ernan and St Monan have all been attributed, but the most likely is St Marnan or Marnoch, a 7th century missionary. A map of Moravia (Moray) from 1642 clearly shows 'Kirk of Langmorn' on the spot. An early chapel on the site is said to have been replaced by a water powered grain mill around the 15th or 16th century.

Until recently, water power was a significant feature of the distillery. A stream, rising in Blackhills and Brown Muir, runs through the site and supplies the cooling water. The same stream also runs through Coleburn, Glen Elgin and Linkwood distilleries before joining the River Lossie. Andy Shand, whose father was distillery manager in the 1970s, remembers fishing for perch in the two distillery pools as a boy and says he hardly ever came away empty handed.

In 1903, it was reported that Longmorn had installed an unusual piece of equipment to dispose of pot ale and spent lees. This was called the Destructor and used waste heat from the still fires to burn off 75 per cent of the liquid waste. There is no record of how long it was in use. In 1919, Longmorn allowed Masataka Taketsuru, a young Japanese chemist, to serve a short apprenticeship. He went on to found the Nikka distilling company, a hugely successful Japanese corporation. In 2001, a malt from their Yoichi distillery won *Whisky Magazine*'s Best of the Best competition, so Taketsuru must have studied hard at Longmorn.

The 1970s saw the distillery increased first to six stills and then to eight. One result of this expansion is that the wash stills are in a separate building from the spirit stills. Malting ceased at Longmorn in 1970 but the stills were coal-fired throughout the decade. A water wheel, powered by the out-flow from the worm tubs, drove a belt drive which turned the switchers and the rummagers in the stills. That water wheel was still on view at the distillery until recently, but sadly has now disappeared. The old steam engine, however, which ceased operation in 1979, is still displayed. The wood from the dismantled washbacks was eventually recycled

as flooring in the garden bar at Chivas Brothers' Linn House in Keith.

Generally speaking, Longmorn is a businesslike distillery these days; no visitors except by appointment. The stills are kept gleaming though and the grounds are tidy and park-like. The railway station and the fixed steam engine form a tantalising link with the past. The name of the site provides a link to a veiled but fascinating time before the distillery existed. From the road near the distillery you can see the modern windmills turning over on Cairn Uish — a link with the future perhaps? How long before we see distilleries with their own wind turbines?

This is a whisky which ages well. The current official expression is a 15 year old but Longmorn is readily available from independent bottlers and its reputation is in no doubt; it is highly valued by blenders and is commonly referred to as a 'top dressing'. Most of the annual output of 3.5 million litres is used for blending. Lord Sainsbury claimed that his favourite dram was a vatting of Clynelish, Glenlivet and Longmorn, and David Daiches, in *Scotch Whisky*, describes how in 1967 he was given a sample at the distillery from a cask that was filled in 1899. It was the oldest whisky he had ever tasted, at 68 years old. He was surprised that there was any whisky in the cask at all, and also that it was still mellow and pleasant.

Recently, I shared a few drams of 36 year old Longmorn (SMWS bottling) with an old friend from Copenhagen. It was distilled in December 1968 and we both found ourselves animated and reflective, cheered and wistful in turns, as the magical stuff whisked us back all the way to our teens. The deep mahogany dram was a delight on the nose, with pineapple and paint, cigar boxes, orange-scented cedar, plum jam, leather, redcurrants, gingerbread and garden bonfires. The taste was of rich fruit cake, banana loaf, puff candy and treacle toffee. A stoater of a dram — but it was the long years invested in that delicious nectar that triggered the emotions most.

Another time I had the pleasure of a vertical tasting of Longmorn at the distillery with Colin Scott, head blender with Chivas Brothers. Colin led us through the new-make spirit, to cask samples at 15 years old from a bourbon barrel, a remade hogshead and a sherry butt, which are the components of the 15 year old Longmorn single malt. That is a lovely

dram, definitely more than the sum of its parts and a fine example of the blender's art. We then tried the Cask Strength edition, which is 17 years old and 58.3 per cent abv. The tasting was rounded off by a 1969 sample, drawn from a cask. That was perfumed and floral, like a lady's handbag, with nutty sweetness, resin and spice in the flavour and a wisp of smoke at the end; elegance with sinews. I had to agree with Dominic Roskrow (editor of *Whisky Magazine*), who was standing next to me, when he said, 'It doesn't get any better than this!'

LAN MOGAN!

WHAT'S IN A NAME?

One hot day in 625 AD, St Marnoch set off on the road south to Dalriada, after spending a busy fortnight converting the heathen Picts of Moray. Feeling thirsty, he stopped off at the Thunderton House public house in Elgin and was introduced to the delights of mogan — a whisky distilled from malted oats.

Many hours later, he resumed his journey in the company of a Briton, who was returning to Strathclyde from a business trip. But St Marnoch was feeling decidedly the worse for wear after imbibing rather too freely, and about three miles down the road he fell to the ground, salivating and twitching uncontrollably.

The Briton decided to go in search of a monastery for help, so he hailed a passing Pict to ascertain where he was, in order to give the monastic ambulance service directions. 'What is this place called?' he asked. Unfortunately the Pict had a slender command of the Briton's language and believed that the Briton had asked, 'What is wrong with him?' Studying the sozzled saint closely, he replied, 'Lan mogan' — which means, 'Full of oat whisky'.

The Briton hurried off and quickly found a monastery occupied by the local chapter of the Knights Hospitaller. But the monks had never heard of a place called Fullofoatwhisky, and were unable to find the saint for many hours. St Marnoch, alone and denied succour, had expired before they reached him. As a warning to others, the spot where he died became known as Lanmogan, and over the years it evolved to become Longmorn.

When John Duff built his distillery in 1894, he called it Longmorn. Because it is... er... full of whisky.

Iain Russell

MANNOCHMORE

MANNOCHMORE, MEANING 'The Great Place of the Monks', was built in 1971 by Scottish Malt Distillers Ltd, though the licence was held by John Haig & Sons, the oldest distilling family in Scotland. SMD seem to have had a policy at this time of extending existing distilleries by building new plants on the old sites. They did this, for example, at Linkwood, Teaninich, Glendullan and Clynelish. Mannochmore distillery was built immediately adjacent to Glenlossie. The two distilleries are quite separate, though they share the on-site warehousing and dark grains plant. Nonetheless, they are operated as one distilling unit and are operated by the same management and staff. For a while they were operated in monthly rotation.

Some sources say that the two distilleries have different water supplies but it seems likely that both draw water from the springs that rise out of Birnie Moss to the south; water which gathers mainly into the burns of Bardon and Gedloch, though since these are separated from the distilleries by a watershed and run away into the Lossie, the supply must be piped. A smaller burn runs through the distillery, eventually flowing through Linkwood distillery and into the Lossie on the other side of Elgin.

Mannochmore was designed along similar lines to Glenlossie. Both distilleries have six stills and they are quite comparable in shape, though those at Mannochmore do not have purifiers, so the spirit produced has a slightly more robust character. Mannochmore's spirit stills are larger, which might compensate somewhat for the lack of purifiers. Both have eight larch washbacks, Mannochmore's being slightly larger. The Mannochmore mash tun is a cast iron full lauter tun with a domed copper canopy.

Mannochmore produces about 2.6 million litres each year, almost entirely for blending, probably mainly into the Haig and Dimple blends. The Flora and Fauna series shows the great spotted woodpecker on the label and the company has released an edition under the Rare Malts label. Some independent bottlings exist. I have written tasting notes of four cask bottlings for the Scotch Malt Whisky Society and the headlines were 'Summery and Stimulating', 'Burnt Heather Dipped in Syrup', 'Fun-Provoking' and 'Explosive and Tooth-Searing'. These were all obviously delightful drams in their own individual ways, which makes it difficult to understand the logic of putting Mannochmore into the infamous Loch Dhu.

LOCH DHU

During the 1990s, UDV were at the forefront of producing some experimental whisky drinks. These included Bell's Red Devil (chilli flavoured whisky) and a whisky mixed with Irn Bru. Loch Dhu ('Black Loch') was also released. This was a black whisky, which, like most of the other experiments, was aimed at a younger market. The marketing assumption here would be that young consumers are more experimental in their choices. Unkind persons might suggest that the assumption was that young consumers are just more gullible — though not that gullible apparently, because none of the new drinks sold and they were all eventually abandoned.

I first encountered Loch Dhu at a tasting during Scotsfest in New York in 1998. It was one of the whiskies imported by Schieffelin & Somerset, who were co-sponsors of the festival, a precursor of Tartan Day. Loch Dhu is also the name of a salmon fly and I immediately knew why the whisky was named after it as my first reaction was to spit it out and get away — but it wasn't that easy. Its evil Fernet Branca–like taste had barbed into my mouth and left my face twisted for half an hour.

The creators of Loch Dhu were very reluctant to say how it was made. It was definitely Mannochmore 10 year old, but they said the black colour was achieved mainly through heavy charring. Others have claimed that it owed more to very heavy dosing, if not

adulteration, with spirit caramel, otherwise known as E150. Rumour also has it that part of the reason it was withdrawn was that the Scotch Whisky Association forced it off the market for not conforming to the law that whisky must have only three simple ingredients, so much caramel was there in the mix.

Incredibly, some people liked it. It was particularly popular in Denmark, where people have long enjoyed salty liquorice with their strong black coffee. So much so that someone in Denmark has tried to fill the gap left by Loch Dhu with Cu Dhub, a very similar black whisky based on product from Speyside distillery. Cu Dhub seems to be heading for even more vilification than Loch Dhu, which nonetheless has somehow become a bit of a cult whisky, with its gothic horror nature and its rarity value. It now regularly sells for £170 a bottle and I heard it was fetching up to $1,000 in the US; black market whisky indeed.

Here are a few comments gleaned from the web, which will give those who have never tried it a suggestion of its quality:

'Awful.'

'Blatantly offensive.'

'Tastes like cigar ashes mixed with vodka and mouldy blackberry jam.'

'Nauseating.'

'Unbelievable that it was commercially marketed.'

'Tastes… contaminated.'

'There's no accounting for taste.'

'Overwhelmed with E150 caramel colouring.'

'Horrid.'

'Scary.'

'Run away!'

'Aqua crematoria! Only malt I ever threw down the sink.'

'A freak of a drink.'

'The unpleasant nose is not so bad compared to the really awful taste.'

'Like licking an ashtray.'

'Really filthy stuff.'

'The absolute worst single malt I've ever tasted.'

'An insult to my taste buds.'

'For the first time in living memory, I did not finish the glass and had to offend the host.'

MILTONDUFF

MILTONDUFF WAS AMONG THE earliest of the Speyside distilleries, one of the clutch of distilleries licensed in the months after the Excise Act of 1823. There is a pretty strong likelihood that most of these distilleries were already in existence and merely became legalised. Miltonduff was actually founded in 1824 by Andrew Peary and Robert Bain. It was built on the site of, or indeed incorporated the remains of, the old meal mill, which had belonged to Pluscarden Priory.

The priory was established by King Alexander II in 1230. By that time, nearby Elgin had already had its impressive cathedral for a hundred years. Pluscarden was an important religious site during the middle ages and was undoubtedly a significant feature in the lives of the people in the area. One of the things the Benedictine monks were expert at was brewing and they are reputed to have used the water of the Black Burn for more than just turning the mill to crush the meal; they also used it to make high quality ale from the excellent local barley. In the 19th century, Pluscarden Priory had been an abandoned ruin for some time. Alfred Barnard was clearly regaled with the story of the monks and their alcoholic beverages. It is worth quoting him in full because he tells it so well:

The monks of Pluscarden, among other things, were adept in the art of brewing fine ales, the quality of which was considered to be superior to any in Scotland. It was so good that it —

'Made the hearts of all rejoice, and filled
The Abbey with unutterable bliss;
Raised their devotions to that pitch
That Heldon's Hills echo'd their hallelujahs.'

They brewed their ales and made their drinks from the waters of the Black Burn, a rivulet that descends from the mossy uplands of the Black Hills and runs through the plain, and which every storm converts into a torrent. Of this stream the following legend is told:— On a New Year's Day in the 15th century, an imposing ceremony occurred on the grounds where now stands Milton Duff. It was the occasion of blessing the waters of the Black Burn, previous to its being used by the Benedictine Monks of Pluscarden. Attended by his priors, palmers and priests, an aged abbot proceeded to the banks of the stream, where, kneeling on a stone with hands outstretched to heaven, he invoked a blessing on its waters, and ever after the life-giving beverage distilled therefrom was christened 'aqua vitae', the rivulet being to this day held in high repute and veneration by the natives. We were shown the stone on which the abbot is said to have knelt; it bears an indistinct date, and is built into the wall of the Malt Mill.

That is quite a story, and indeed the stone is still there. Barnard is in no doubt that the monks were making whisky as well as ale (remember, the very first recorded reference to whisky-making in Scotland names the distiller as Friar John Corr). I'd often wondered why so many men wanted to become monks in the middle ages; now I begin to understand. Barnard gives us the often quoted fact that 'at one time there were as many as 50 illicit stills in the Glen of Pluscarden', something which is hard to dispute when he goes on to say that 'there are those living who remember many of them in operation'.

At the time of Barnard's visit, the distillery was owned by William Stuart, who also owned, or at least occupied, 'the Old House of Milton Duff'. Barnard and his party were invited to explore the house and he describes it as 'one of the most curious and interesting dwellings we have ever visited.' Before moving on to the distillery they were regaled with 'a nip of creamy Old Milton Duff Whisky'; it is quite unusual for Barnard even to mention whisky, let alone describe it, and having a dram before the distillery visit shows William Stuart to be a man of some generosity and urbanity.

Barnard says of the distillery, 'the appearance of Milton Duff is a complete contrast to the other distilleries in the district. There is scarcely a building alike,

and they are all, with one exception, detached.' Today's Miltonduff distillery still has a somewhat rambling appearance, though a lot of water from the Black Burn has flowed under the bridge since Barnard visited the place. It is now one of the biggest distilleries in the area, with an annual production capacity of 5.5 million litres (compared to about 350,000 litres in 1886). How did it get from there to here?

Pearey and Bain established it but ten years later Bain dropped out of the picture. Pearey sold out to William Stuart in 1866. Stuart was also a co-owner of Highland Park distillery, and Barnard reported that Milton Duff only used peat imported from Orkney for their kilning, because Orkney peats 'are said to be the finest in the kingdom.' In Barnard's day, Milton Duff had a wash still and a spirit still but operated triple distillation. The distillery was extended in 1897, bringing the capacity up to 750,000 litres. In 1936, Hiram Walker, with the help of Ballantine's James Barclay, purchased Miltonduff and its near neighbour, Glenburgie. The distillery was modernised at that time.

In 1964, a pair of Lomond stills was installed at Miltonduff and the name of the whisky they produced was Mosstowie. In 1974/75, the number of stills was increased to six and, in 1981, the Lomond stills were removed and replaced with traditional swan neck stills, though these were built incorporating the bases of the Lomond stills. It remains the case that two of the stills have much deeper bases than the others, for that reason. Miltonduff is one of the few distilleries to have a spirit still with a viewing window, which is always fascinating to see. There was a further refurbishment in 1999/2000.

Miltonduff now runs 40 mashes in a seven-day working week, using two waters and a continuous sparge process. Milling and mashing are completely computer controlled. Water from the Black Burn, which rushes by the distillery, is still used to cool the condensers, but production water is drawn from 120 feet deep boreholes (hard water with minerals). There are 16 stainless steel washbacks and even at seven-day production they manage to have 57 hour fermentation. There is considerable warehousing at Miltonduff (68,000 casks) and all spirit goes into first fill bourbon barrels.

Not much is available as single malt, unfortunately, though Gordon & MacPhail bottle a number of expressions. Miltonduff, along with Glenburgie, has long been an important component of Ballantine's. It also goes into an export blend called Old Smuggler. The company bottles a 15 year old, which is sweet and fruity on the palate and has a fragrance of quince, nut oil and Liquorice Allsorts.

In 2005, the distillery unwittingly took delivery of four loads of peated barley. The fact was not discovered until mashing had taken place, so there may well be a batch of peated Miltonduff somewhere, though it is not yet known what the company will do with these casks.

In the 1940s, Benedictine monks moved back into Pluscarden Priory and began a lengthy process of restoration. In 1974 the priory was elevated to the status of abbey but, as far as I know, the monks have not yet returned to making ale from the water of the Black Burn.

SCOTCH DRINK (Extract)

Robert Burns

Thou art the life o' public haunts;
But thee, what were our fairs and rants?
Ev'n godly meetings o' the saunts,
By thee inspir'd,
When gaping they besiege the tents,
Are doubly fir'd.

That merry night we get the corn in!
O sweetly then thou reams the horn in!
Or reekin' on a New–Year mornin'
In cog or bicker,
An' just a wee drap sp'ritual burn in,
An' gusty sucker!

KEITH

Keith, a market town on the River Isla, proclaims itself
'the friendly town'. Its oldest part, known as Fife Keith, dates from
the 12th century. It is home to a tartan museum and the
Keith Folk Festival. It is in the most easterly part of Speyside
and shares some of the outlook and Doric accent of the
Banffshire and Buchan north east corner.

AULTMORE
GLEN KEITH
GLENTAUCHERS
STRATHISLA
STRATHMILL

Photo: Robin Laing

AULTMORE

ONE OF THOSE BEAUTIFUL back roads undiscovered by most travellers runs north from Keith towards Buckie and the coast. A couple of miles along this road (the B9016) from Keith lies the distillery of Aultmore. It would have been even more of a back road in the early nineteenth century and the wild Foggie Moss to the east, with its burns and springs, was a notorious haunt of illicit whisky distillers. The Foggie Moss now supplies the distillery's water.

Aultmore, which commenced production in 1897, was built in the late Victorian whisky boom by Alexander Edward (who had also built Craigellachie distillery). It had about two years of promising production and a growing reputation when, in 1899, the collapse of Pattison's of Leith threw it into a spin. It stumbled on until after the First World War; then, in 1923, it was sold to Dewar's. A couple of years later, Dewar's became part of the Distillers Company Limited. Dewar's was later acquired by the Bacardi Corporation, in 1998, and Aultmore was one of the distilleries to go with it.

Various improvements took place in the 1960s, and in 1971 the distillery was largely rebuilt and expanded from two stills to four. Part of this rebuilding involved the retirement of the old steam engine, a 10 horse power engine built by James Abernethy of Aberdeen in 1898. It had powered the barley and malt conveyers and elevators, the malt dresser and mill, the mashing processes, the wash still

rummager and several pumps for more than 70 years. It now has pride of place in the new Aultmore distillery, visible through a large window from the main courtyard, a testament to the engineering achievements of the past — now superseded, but immensely important in their day.

At Aultmore, the old sits side by side with the new. The still-house dates from the reconstruction of 1971 and has more recently been fitted (like the one at Craigellachie) with three large roller windows. They make the stills nicely visible and help to control the temperature (mainly for the comfort of the stillman), but their main function is to allow access when stills or parts of stills need to be replaced. At other distilleries, this frequently involves the removal of roof sections — at Aultmore it is relatively trouble free.

Other evidence of investment at Aultmore since the take-over by Bacardi can be seen. The destoner looks like something Luke Skywalker might fly and the new gleaming stainless steel mash tun, installed in 2003, is also like something out of *Star Wars*. This full-lauter mash tun was built and supplied by Steineker of Freising (near Munich). The cost of having it installed, since it needed to be housed in a new building, would have been in the region of £1.5m.

Douglas Milne, the distillery's, administrator, has been at Aultmore since 1962. He believes it was much the same then as it had been in 1897. He has therefore seen many changes, but he vividly recalls the day the new mash tun arrived from Germany on fourteen articulated trucks. It was constructed and fitted on-site without any real hitch, but as soon as it went into production there were teething problems.

When the night shift staff could not get the grist into the tun they called out Douglas, who, in desperation, contacted Steineker. They did their troubleshooting by controlling a full mash cycle from their own computer in Germany through a modem. This is the kind of technology that hints at a future where distilleries can be controlled from a central nerve centre by remote computer link, requiring no distilling staff at all.

In another sign of the times, Aultmore is a distillery with no whisky. The warehouses (as at Craigellachie) were removed a few years ago and new spirit is tankered away from the site to Cambus, where its fate is largely unknown to the distillery personnel. What is known is that the largest share of the two million litres annual output goes into blends. A small amount is put aside to be laid down as Aultmore single malt, currently being bottled at 12 years old.

I have not tasted the current distillery

bottling but I have tried a number of cask strength expressions from the Scotch Malt Whisky Society. These have tended to show recurring themes of toffee, chocolate raisins and citric notes in the nose, and the taste is always deliciously hot. A recent example of a tasting note I wrote for a 14 year old had the title 'Giddy and Voluptuous'.

GIDDY AND VOLUPTUOUS

This harvest gold sample is from a refill barrel. The nose has a giddy blend of creamy toffee, butterscotch, golden syrup and straw bales. Reduced, it seems deeper but still clean, with fruit pastilles, honey on buttered toast and cocoa — a real bedtime whisky. The neat taste is simply delicious, with breath-taking heat and malt, spice and dark chocolate on the palate. Even diluted it remains a perfect balance of syrupy textures, with ginger and cinnamon and a lingering finish. A voluptuous whisky experience.

GLEN KEITH

EVERY DISTILLERY SEEMS TO have its claim to fame. Glen Keith started life as the Glen Keith-Glenlivet distillery in 1958. Built by Chivas Brothers, it was the first new distillery in Speyside in the 20th century, so much had the trauma of the Pattison's crash stunned the industry. It was a radical conversion of an old meal mill, the Mill of Keith.

Glen Keith lies in the town of Keith just downstream from Strathisla distillery and just upstream from Chivas' Linn House, so named because it looks over a waterfall of the River Isla below the two distilleries. Next door to Glen Kieth is the oldest building in the town, Milton Tower. This was originally part of the Castle of Milton, built by George Ogilvie in 1480. The castle walls towered by the riverside, overlooking a deep pool known as the Linn Pot. At one time a part of the castle fell into the river, taking some treasure with it, which local legend says still lies in the depths of this dark, swirling basin.

Chivas Brothers wanted a light, smooth malt to use in blends and so, unusually, the distillery was set up with three stills and a triple distillation, though they alternated between triple and double distillation so that the distillery was in effect producing two different types of spirit. In 1970, two new stills were added to increase production and after that, double distillation was the norm. A sixth still was installed in 1983. It was during the 1970 expansion that Glen Keith became the first malt distillery to have gas heated stills. Indeed, in the late 1970s, Glen Keith was also a pioneer of computerised, automated systems for milling, mashing and distilling.

It is sad, therefore, to see the distillery lying silent now, with an abandoned feel to it and light showing through the Oregon pine washbacks where they have dried out and split. Though the distillery is officially closed, it seems to be in fairly good condition; certainly the stills are in place and gleaming. Part of the building now houses the Chivas laboratories. New spirit from nearby Strathisla distillery is piped over to Glen Keith, where it is poured into tankers and taken to the Keith No 2 bond. This reduces the number of heavy vehicles that need to negotiate the very cramped space at Strathisla distillery.

There is still some stock of Glen Keith around, though I believe they stopped bottling the single malt recently. That was only available from 1994 anyway, so it will become quite rare. Most of the output of this distillery went into blends,

concentrated at the distillery to make it even peatier. Some of this concentrated peaty water was apparently sent to Japan, causing suspicion among the Customs and Excise staff at Heathrow. This sounds like a tall story but it comes from a reliable source.

KENTUCKY KITTY

It was in the yard at Glen Keith that Dizzy the cat was discovered on 15 June 1993, after her famous trip from Kentucky in a consignment of bourbon barrels. Staff heard the noise of some kind of animal inside the container and called the SSPCA, who suggested drilling a hole and killing the unknown creature with gas. It was decided, however, to take a chance and have a look, and out staggered the weak and wobbly Dizzy, who had spent more than four weeks in there without food. The distillery workers wanted to keep the cat but she first had to spend six months in quarantine. She then spent some time at the home of one of the distillery workers but when he separated from his wife, Dizzy was brought back to Glen Keith and later moved to Strathisla distillery. At Strathisla, her name was apparently changed to Passport. I am told the cat is no longer at Strathisla but is still alive and well, living in the area, after no doubt spreading her Kentucky genes around the neighbourhood.

mainly Chivas Regal and Passport. I had my first chance to taste the 10 year old Glen Keith single malt while staying at Chivas' Craigduff House nearby. I thought it had a menthol, slightly mouth-numbing effect. Unfortunately, I did not have enough to experience the head-numbing effect.

There is another Craigduff connection: Glen Keith was apparently the source of a curious malt called Craigduff, bottled by Signatory in the early 1970s. This was a peated malt, produced using peated barley from Glen Keith's own maltings (it had a Saladin maltings facility until 1976) and peaty water. The peaty water was brought from Stornoway and

GLENTAUCHERS

GLENTAUCHERS DISTILLERY LIES ABOUT a mile from Mulben on the road to Keith. Gliding along the A95 in a convoy of Audi cars (belonging to Chivas employees, not me), I was admiring the forested hillsides and reflecting on how getting around the area has changed since Barnard was there. Shortly after Maggieknockater, we turned a corner and found that a knacker's wagon had lost a wheel and was hanging off the verge. Its load had partly spilled and several dead cows and horses were lying at the side of the road, while the driver and someone with a tractor were trying to get things righted. It seemed somehow like a scene from Victorian days and I realised that some things change more slowly than others.

I was on my way to visit the distillery, which, for many years, was the spiritual home of Buchanan's famous Black and White blend — the one that featured the two wee terriers, one Scottish and one West Highland, wonderfully drawn by American artist Morgan Dennis.

James Buchanan was born in Canada in 1849. His parents, Scottish emigrants, returned to Scotland one year later. In 1879, he started working in the whisky business as London agent for Mackinlays of Leith. Five years later, financed by his supplier, W. P. Lowrie of Glasgow, he set up his own business and started producing and marketing The Buchanan Blend. This was a great success, particularly in various overseas markets, and within 15 years it had become one of the big three blended whisky brands. In 1897, to ensure supplies of malt for the blend, James built Glentauchers distillery in partnership with W. P. Lowrie.

The Buchanan Blend won an exclusive contract with the House of Commons and changed its name to House of Commons. However, the members got into the habit of referring to it by the colour of its label — Black and White. Soon after, Buchanan bowed to the inevitable and changed the name again. That became the registered trademark in 1904. In 1906, W.P. Lowrie retired and full ownership of Glentauchers passed to James Buchanan. In 1915, Buchanan & Co Ltd merged with Dewar's, and then, in 1925, along with Johnnie Walker, they were amalgamated into DCL.

James Buchanan became a very rich and successful whisky baron. In 1920 he was offered a peerage by Lloyd George, becoming Lord Woolavington of Lavington in return for a substantial donation to the Liberal Party. Being a shrewd customer, he is said to have signed the cheque 'Woolavington' in order that Lloyd George could not renege on the deal. He was made a peer in 1922.

Buchanan and Lowrie chose the site for their distillery partly for its water supply and partly for its proximity to the Inverness to Aberdeen railway. The water comes from the Rosarie and the Tauchers burns, both of which are dammed. The higher dam (Rosarie-fed) provides the process or mashing water. Overflow from that goes into the lower dam (Tauchers-fed), which then provides the cooling water.

In the early days, the water supply was so plentiful that the dam was also able to provide water to drive a turbine that supplied power for the distillery's machinery. The turbine was replaced by a steam engine in 1955.

These days, the distillery finds the summer water supply can be insufficient and it has therefore fitted an internal loop system, which allows some of the water to be recycled. Ironically, although water can be in short supply, the ground around the distillery is quite boggy. The trains still whizz by between Inverness and Aberdeen, but the distillery siding and its puggie have long gone.

Glentauchers was designed by Keith architect John Alcock, under the supervision of the famous Charles Cree Doig of Elgin. It was given twin pagodas, just like Strathisla and Strathmill. The old kiln house is now a store, infested with pigeons, though I understand that there are plans to develop the building. Substantial alterations took place in the 1920s but it was in 1965/66 that the big rebuild happened, increasing the number of stills from two to six. The unusual copper-canopied mash tun was fitted by Abercrombie's at that time.

In 1985, United Distillers, as the company then was,

mothballed the distillery, along with nine others. It was bought by Allied Distillers Ltd in 1989 and reopened. Allied was taken over by Pernod Ricard in 2005.

Glentauchers was one of the first distilleries to pioneer the automated system of cleaning still interiors with caustic, known as CIP (Cleaning in Place). The distillery is unlikely to see any other significant automation for some time. It is deliberately kept as a traditional, manual operation distillery for training purposes. That way, every worker gets to learn about all the stages of the whisky-making process in a hands-on way.

Most of the distillery warehouses have now gone. There are two left, holding about 7,000 casks in total. About 95 per cent of current production is tankered away. There are a few independent bottlings to be found but the vast majority of the 3.1 million litres of annual production goes for blending. That means mainly Teachers and Ballantine's, but quite a lot goes to Diageo, so it may well still be a significant component of Black and White, which incidentally still has the Scottie and Westie on the label.

A WEE DRAP O' WHISKY
(Extract)

Traditional

A wee drap o' whisky I tak' when I'm weary
My blood for to warm and my spirits to cheer
And when I sit doon I intend to be merry
So fill up a bumper and bring it round here.

Come noble waiter; bring in a large measure,
I mean hauf a mutchkin, the best o' the toon
An' when it is drunk, an' it's time to be joggin
Wi' the lightest o' care we'll gang toddlin' hame.

STRATHISLA

STRATHISLA DISTILLERY IS FAMOUS for two things — it is very old and it is very picturesque — oh, and the whisky is quite good, too! The distillery dates from 1786, which makes it the oldest distillery in Speyside and one of the oldest in Scotland. In the 12th and 13th centuries, Dominican monks were using spring water here to brew beer, the first part of the whisky-making process. In 1545, George Ogilvie of Miltown had a grant of lands from the bishop of Moray, including the brasina or brew-house of Keith. That was on the site of this distillery, which has a stone set into the wall with the date 1695 carved on it.

In 1786, the distillery (originally called Milltown) was established by George Taylor and Alexander Milne. It was called Milton when Barnard visited, though he says that its produce was known as Stathisla whisky. It passed to John Macdonald for a few years before being bought by William Longmore in 1830. Jay Pomeroy, a Russian-born financier, took it over in 1946. Five years later he was convicted of tax evasion; the distillery was bought in 1950 by James Barclay for Seagrams and the name was changed to Strathisla. Under Seagrams' ownership, Strathisla became part of the Chivas Brothers group, now owned by Pernod Ricard.

Barnard tells us Keith 'has been the scene of many a sanguinary conflict and romantic episode'; the sanguinary conflicts he tells of relate to Montrose, who came to Keith first as a victor (1646) and later as a captive (1649), and of the 'war-

like Peter Roy Macgregor' who came in 1667 to raid the town. The local inhabitants rose up and confronted Macgregor and his bloodthirsty band as they were 'marching over the "Auld Brig" on to the churchyard, headed by their piper. A well-aimed shot from the churchyard soon silenced the piper and put an end to his music. One of his companions gave his body a kick and sent it over the bridge into the stream, and the pipes, by the compulsive pressure of the dying man, continued to screech out his requiem, until both were silenced by the waters of the Isla.'

When Barnard arrived at Milton (or Strathisla), it was already a hundred years old. He refers to it as having an 'old-world look' and 'possessing the charm of age few others have' (though it is the only Speyside distillery at which he mentions condensers). The rustic, fairy-tale charm of Strathisla nowadays has much to do with the twin pagodas and the water wheel. Though Barnard talks about 'the kilns', his picture shows two vents in the roof, but not pagodas. These were yet to be developed, by Charles Doig, the first being installed at Dailuaine in 1889.

Actually, Strathisla's twin pagodas were designed by another distillery architect, John Alcock. An invitation for estimates to be submitted was placed in the local newspaper in May 1898. Alcock got the commission and work began in June 1898. His design plans for the Strathisla pagodas are kept at the Elgin Library. The fact that the pagodas had a different architect to the rest of Strathisla distillery probably explains their unusual height-to-width ratio. Doig may have had a consulting role.

The pagodas no longer house kilns as malting ceased here in the 1960s, but they have been retained for their obvious character; Strathisla must be the most attractive and photogenic of all the distilleries. I was at an event at the Scotch Malt Whisky Society in London a few years ago, when a woman unveiled a surprise birthday present for her husband. It was a beautiful cake replica of Strathisla distillery: truly, a distillery good enough to eat. Needless to say, a picture of the distillery features on the bottle.

Currently the four stills sit under the pagodas, seeming cramped but somehow full of character as their proud swan necks crane up into the beams and rafters. The wash stills are of the lantern glass design and the spirit stills are dumpier, with boil ball necks. These stills work their magic under ancient beams and produce a new-make spirit, which, I am told, is relatively oily, heavy and robust for a Speyside.

Water for the production comes from the Fons Bulliens well, the same source that supplied the ale-brewing monks of the 12th and 13th centuries. When Barnard visited, he was told the water came from the Broomhill Spring: 'We visited the reservoir, wherein it was collected, said to be haunted nightly by fays and fairies. The water is so bright and clear that a pebble we dropped into it seemed magnified into a huge crystal boulder.' A new water wheel had been built five years earlier by James Abernethy. The River Isla, which flows right through the distillery, has always supplied cooling water. In 2005, Chivas installed a salmon ladder where the distillery bridge runs over a weir.

Strathisla is the backbone of Chivas Regal, which sells a massive four million cases annually worldwide. It also finds its way into other Chivas blends, such as 100 Pipers and, more notably, the prestige brand of Royal Salute, which sells about 100,000 cases annually, mainly in Asia. This deluxe blend was formulated by blender Jimmy Lang in 1953 to commemorate the coronation of Queen Elizabeth. Its name refers to the 21-gun salute that is customary on such state occasions, and the blend was appropriately created as a 21 year old offering. Not every distillery could have created such a thing at short notice (Chivas Brothers only acquired the distillery in 1950) but Strathisla is rich in old stocks of whisky. Even today, it has one of the greatest stocks of long-matured single malt.

Inside one of the warehouses at Strathisla distillery is the Royal Salute vault, where only the luckiest visitors are taken for an atmospheric dram of this most exclusive deluxe blend. On my visit to the vault, I was especially lucky, for not only was I in the hallowed company of many distinguished casks, but also of distinguished whisky writers and Chivas representatives. Together we watched in awe as valinch samples were drawn from the Royal Salute 100 cask selection and, even more excitingly, from a cask of the 38 year old Stone of Destiny blend.

This is an incredibly regal dram, nosing of sherry, rich oak, bicycle tyre repair glue, orange peel and cloves, and with espresso coffee and good chocolate in the taste. This was a whisky moment. Sadly, it was in the morning and at the start of a busy day. It was not therefore my destiny to get stoned on the Stone of Destiny. The group was elated by the whisky but sorry to see some of it poured on the cobbled floor as a libation to the God of Good Whisky, and some poured back in the cask as a canny Scottish wink to posterity.

FIRE AND BRIMSTONE

Health and safety regulations can be seen by many as a hindrance, but there is no doubt that they have reduced the number of incidents which previously occurred with some frequency, endangering life and limb and disrupting production:

DESTRUCTIVE FIRE AT KEITH
Banffshire Journal

Tuesday, 25 January 1876

The town of Keith was on Sunday night the scene of one of the most destructive conflagrations that has ever been witnessed in the district. The fire took place at the buildings connected with Milton Distillery, the property of Mr Wm. Longmore.

About ten minutes past nine o'clock Mr Sellar, the distiller, went to walk round the buildings as usual before retiring for the night. No sooner had he left the house than he became alarmed at a lurid glare and on turning into the square, he saw flames issuing from two windows of the straw room next the threshing mill.

In a very short time an immense concourse of spectators gathered, and applied their energies to the saving of property.

Out of the 66 cows in the byres, 30 perished in the fire, at a loss of £700; along with 500 quarters of barley, an excellent threshing machine and a steam engine were destroyed. The premises were supplied by gas, but this had judiciously been switched off.

The fire, however, did not interfere with the operations at the distillery — no one was injured and no one was thrown out of work.

EXPLOSION AT MILTON DISTILLERY
Banffshire Journal

Tuesday, 8 July 1879

An alarming explosion occurred at Milton Distillery on Saturday morning. Work was started a little after nine o'clock at the Malt Mill which with the Malt Deposit room above and Still-house near-by forms the centre block of the extensive distillery buildings. Three men were employed feeding the mill by conveying malt in barrows from the deposit room when the men observed a flame of fire coming up the elevator which pierced the malt deposit room. The combustible material was quickly ignited and a violent explosion occurred instantaneously. Only one man, John Taylor, was injured, being severely burned in his face.

The explosion caused very considerable damage and was thought to have resulted from a small piece of stone coming in contact with the cylinder [of the mill] and originated a spark which had set fire to the fine, powdery and very explosive substance thrown off by the grain when going through the milling process.

STRATHMILL

STRATHMILL DISTILLERY IS NOW the home of Diageo's Heritage Visits Team. Sadly, that does not mean that it is any easier for ordinary mortals to get shown around. Strathmill is still very much closed to visitors and has the same unwelcoming, fortress feel as most of the company's Speyside distilleries. Whisky anoraks wander around outside, like the adventurers in the tale of the Sleeping Beauty, wondering if there is a way through the mass of briers and whether the legends they have heard might be true.

So what does a Heritage Visits Team do? According to the company's website, the team 'works with markets from around the world in designing and arranging visits to Scotland, to build relationships with customers, inform and educate sales teams, offer incentives to consumers and grow our Scottish brands throughout the Diageo world.' So, unless you are part of 'the Diageo world', which doesn't seem to include end customers — forget it.

Strathmill distillery, as the name suggests, was once a mill, and is naturally situated on the bank of the River Isla, on the southern edge of Keith. It was converted from a corn mill in 1891, though it seems that the building had previously been turned into a distillery in 1823. That whisky incarnation only lasted for four years and the distilling equipment was dismantled in 1837. The 1823 distillery was known as Strathisla, as the mill had been called Strathisla Mills (of course, at

that time the distillery we now know as Strathisla was still called Milton). In 1891 it was called Glenisla-Glenlivet but the name changed to Strathmill in 1895, when it was acquired by Gilbey's of London. Confused?

The distillery is wedged between the river and the Keith-Dufftown railway in a pleasantly wooded setting. Just downriver from Strathmill is Keith's Auld Brig. This packhorse bridge, dating from 1609, is the oldest remaining bridge in Banffshire and one of the oldest in Scotland. It was erected by Thomas Murray and his wife, Janet Lindsay, in memory of their son, who drowned while trying to cross the river. In 1770 it was replaced by the more substantial Union Bridge, which still carries the main road. Under the Auld Brig is Campbells' Hole — reputedly once a tunnel linking to Milton Tower. The name arose because some Campbells, fleeing Jacobite forces, hid there in 1746.

It is not recorded whether they were discovered. Under the Union Bridge is a deep pool known as the Gaun's Pot, where witches were regularly drowned until that practice ceased in 1735.

Just upstream one finds Brandy Brae, which apparently got its name from an incident in which a smuggler's cart, loaded with brandy, accidentally tipped and spilled its casks down the brae. It is hard to imagine why anyone would be smuggling brandy into Keith, but there you are. In fact, Strathmill distillery is fabled to have kept a whisky fountain, supplying an endless flow of whisky for the benefit of visitors. Unfortunately this fountain no longer exists, though it would be a real public relations scoop for any distillery that could persuade Customs and Excise to allow a revival of the tradition. Certainly, with a whisky fountain, who would need to smuggle brandy?

Following the Isla upstream a couple of miles, one comes to Towiemore, site of a distillery that operated between 1896 and 1930, and whose whisky was notorious for turning cloudy when water was added. Even further upstream is Drummuir Castle, a fabulous Victorian edifice, which is Diageo's 'Home of Scotch Whisky on Speyside'.

Keith, like many centres of distillation, seems to have quite a history of connection with holy men. The town itself is dedicated to St Rufus, or more properly St Maelrubha of Applecross, who came here as a missionary in 700 AD. Early on, the town was known as Kethmalruff, and the present-day church of St Rufus is close to the Auld Brig. In 1195, Keith was included in a charter of lands granted by King William the Lion to the Abbey of Kinloss and it was probably at this time that the monks started serious brewing activity in the town. John Ogilvie, born in Keith in 1579, converted to Catholicism and worked in Scotland as an undercover Jesuit priest, before he was captured, tortured, condemned for treason and hanged in Glasgow on 10 March 1615. Ogilvie, canonised on 17 October 1976, is Scotland's only post-Reformation Saint,

and indeed the first Scot to be canonised for over 700 years.

By the way, did you know that Gordon Bennett, the American playboy whose name became a mild expletive, came from Keith?

A major expansion at Strathmill took place in 1968, when the number of stills was increased from two to four and purifiers were added. The present manager, Randolph Winchester, started working there in 1959. He has seen the change from direct-firing of stills to steam heating; he has seen the disappearance of the cooperage and the maltings. He has had to clean the insides of Oregon pine washbacks with heather besoms before they were replaced with stainless steel vessels. Many other changes of equipment and distilling methods have taken place in Randolph's time at Strathmill.

The distillery is currently operated by Justerini & Brooks and nearly all of the output goes into J&B Rare. J&B requires light, gentle malts, and these are achieved at Strathmill by plenty of reflux in the boil ball stills. Unexpectedly, about 37 per cent of the spirit is matured in sherry casks and Michael Jackson calls Strathmill single malt 'the whisky world's answer to orange muscat'. Very few people get to try it however, beyond the usual Flora and Fauna edition (in this case, the label is appropriately graced by the pie-eyed wagtail), some independents and a very rare bottling of 25 year old Strathmill, which marked the distillery's centenary and was only made available to staff and special friends of the company.

SCOTCH DRINK (Extract)

Robert Burns

When neibors anger at a plea,
An' just as wud as wud can be,
How easy can the barley-bree
Cement the quarrel!
It's aye the cheapest lawyers fee
To taste the barrel.

ROTHES

The town of Rothes, about 10 miles south of Elgin,
has an important cluster of distilleries on the lower stretch
of the River Spey. Rothes Castle dates from the year 1200.
It became the seat of the Leslie family, who became
the Earls of Rothes.

**AUCHROISK
CAPERDONICH
COLEBURN
FORSYTHS COPPERSMITHS
GLEN GRANT
GLEN SPEY
GLENROTHES
SPEYBURN**

Photo: Robin Laing

AUCHROISK

DURING THE LATE 1960s and early 1970s, sales of the J&B Rare brand were running high. Justerini & Brooks (a subsidiary of IDV) cranked up production at various distilleries to try and meet this demand but eventually they decided that a new distillery was needed. J&B Rare is a particularly light blend and plenty of light character malt was required. The hunt was on to find a suitable site. Almost accidentally, a spring, called Dorie's Well, was discovered in a gully. It was not the most accessible, but it produced plenty of good, clear, soft water — ideal for the purpose — so IDV bought the land and the water rights immediately.

Westminster Design Associates were commissioned to design and build a large scale distillery that would not be a blot on the landscape. They came up with a complex, completed in 1974, that is modern and spacious while still in the Scottish vernacular style. The white, harled walls and dark slate roofs present a clean, two tone exterior. The different component parts of the complex vary in size and shape, including an odd wee 'Hagrid's hut' type of tower with a steeply conical roof. The variety and multi-dimensional appearance gives an organic, eye-pleasing aesthetic; the design won a Saltire Society award.

John Hughes described Auchroisk as 'one of the last great distillery developments in Scotland.' Most of the new distilleries of recent years have been relatively modest in scale; not so Auchroisk. It has a high powered, six-roller Buhler mill,

eight stainless steel washbacks of 51,000 litre capacity each, eight tall and substantial stills providing a possible annual output of up to four million litres and enough warehouse capacity (265,000 casks) for the equivalent of more than 10 years' production. This is a big distillery, yet it is spacious inside and gives the impression that it was been designed to allow further expansion if required.

These days, Auchroisk is a very well maintained and attractive site and VIP guests are often shown around. It is spotlessly clean, with gleaming copper and stainless steel equipment, meticulously tended lawns and a charming old steam engine proudly on show in the entrance hall. The steam engine previously worked at Strathmill, which, with Glen Spey and Knockando, makes up the Justerini & Brooks (Scotland) Ltd stable of distilleries.

The stills are lofty, lantern shaped, with horizontal lyne arms; all features which will encourage a fine, light spirit. That spirit is then mostly matured in bourbon casks to provide the ideal malt component for J&B blended whisky. However, about 10 per cent of production is rounded off in oloroso butts and sold as a single malt. For a long time this was labeled 'The Singleton', with 'of Auchroisk' in smaller letters below. Recently it seems the owners have dropped 'The Singleton' and they currently sell straightforward Auchroisk. Indeed, Diageo have lifted 'The Singleton' and applied it to some other brands that it wants to give more impetus to, including Dufftown and Glen Ord.

It was said that the 'Singleton' appellation (supposedly meaning a one-off cask, which this is clearly not) was employed because Auchroisk is one of the most difficult of the Gaelic whisky names to pronounce. It is generally accepted that the name means 'the ford across the red stream' (if you believe that two syllables sounding like a snake choking on a fish bone can convey so much poetry) but there is very little agreement about how it should be pronounced and Gaelic scholars, whisky brokers and locals have frequently engaged each other in unseemly rammies, stramashes and collieshangies with hardly a drop being consumed.

None of this reflects on the quality of the dram, which is unquestioned. Auchroisk has won a very impressive number of medals, gongs and awards over the years. About 12 years ago, I clutched a bottle under my arm when I went a-courting. It turned out to be a perfect courting whisky — smooth and sophisticated, easy-drinking and moreish without distracting too much attention from the task at hand. We are now married and The Singleton of Auchroisk must take some of the blame for that.

OH, STEER HER UP AND HAUD HER GAUN

Robert Burns

Oh, steer her up, and haud her gaun —
Her mither's at the mill, jo,
An gin she winna tak a man
E'en let her tak her will, jo.
First shore her wi a gentle kiss,
And ca' another gill, jo,
An gin she tak the thing amiss,
E'en let her flyte her fill, jo.

CAPERDONICH

CAPERDONICH, MEANING EITHER 'secret well' or 'Sunday well', is one of the springs that feed into the Glen Grant Burn, which supplies the water for both Glen Grant and Caperdonich distilleries. An old legend says that it will never run dry. Unfortunately it did run dry in the hot summer of 1976, but that was the first time for 136 years so the legend may not be far off the mark.

This distillery was created by Major James Grant in 1897 and completed in 1898, the last of the Rothes distilleries to be built. At that time, Glen Grant was struggling to keep up with demand and the preferred solution was to build the new distillery, then called Glen Grant No 2, directly across the street. The distillery was intended to be an adjunct to Glen Grant. The stills were copies, using the same purifiers, and the water source was the same. About one-third of the malted barley came from Glen Grant and the rest was brought in, to careful specification.

At the insistence of the Customs and Excise, the spirit produced by Glen Grant No 2 had to be piped over to Glen Grant and filled there. The pipe, which linked the distilleries across the main road, was known locally as 'the whisky pipe' and stories are told about the strenuous and occasionally successful efforts made by local lads to drill and tap it to create another 'secret well'. The pipe did not grace the High Street for very long because the Pattison's crash knocked back

demand for malt whisky and Glen Grant No 2 closed in 1902, after only four years operation. Incredibly, the distillery was mothballed for 63 years, during which time most of the useful machinery found its way back to Glen Grant.

In 1965 the whisky market was buoyant once more and Glen Grant No 2 was reopened, in what must have effectively been a rebuild. Glenlivet and Glen Grant Distilleries Ltd once again fitted it with stills that replicated those at Glen Grant. However, this time it had a different name and Caperdonich was born. Two years later, it was decided to double the capacity by building a second pair of stills. The distillery worked away for 37 years until Pernod Ricard took over Seagrams and closed a handful of the group's distilleries.

Caperdonich remains mothballed but is in reasonably good condition; the paint is peeling in places and the stirring gear in the empty mash tun is rusty, but it seems that all the equipment is there. What will the future hold? Perhaps that

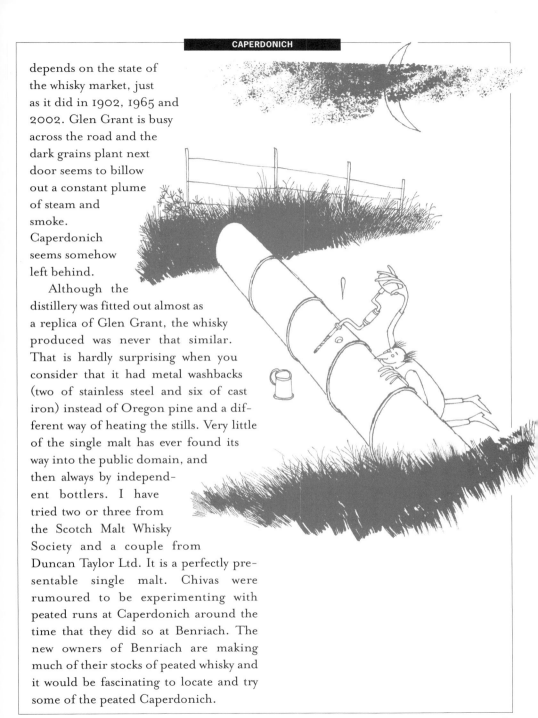

depends on the state of the whisky market, just as it did in 1902, 1965 and 2002. Glen Grant is busy across the road and the dark grains plant next door seems to billow out a constant plume of steam and smoke. Caperdonich seems somehow left behind.

Although the distillery was fitted out almost as a replica of Glen Grant, the whisky produced was never that similar. That is hardly surprising when you consider that it had metal washbacks (two of stainless steel and six of cast iron) instead of Oregon pine and a different way of heating the stills. Very little of the single malt has ever found its way into the public domain, and then always by independent bottlers. I have tried two or three from the Scotch Malt Whisky Society and a couple from Duncan Taylor Ltd. It is a perfectly presentable single malt. Chivas were rumoured to be experimenting with peated runs at Caperdonich around the time that they did so at Benriach. The new owners of Benriach are making much of their stocks of peated whisky and it would be fascinating to locate and try some of the peated Caperdonich.

THE SECRET WELL

Robin Laing

Loons is loons the warld 'roond
But Rothes loons is buggers
The whisky pipe got drilled one night
And the hale toon gathered roond
The pipe got drilled, and the pots got filled,
And they a' got fu' thegither

Major Grant was a decent soul
And the toonfolk loved him well
So why they did this terrible thing
Not one of them could tell
But whisky flowing through a pipe
Suspended in mid-air
Was just a touch temptation
More than some of them could bear

Loons is loons...

Some men dream of a bottle of drams
Some men dream of a still

But what could please a body more
Than an auger and a drill
You'd never need to do any work
And neither buy nor sell
But just enjoy the trickle and flow
Of your very own 'secret well'

Loons is loons...

But the Rothes loons upset the Lord
Wi' their wicked, sinful deeds
An' retribution came to them a'
In the form of achin' heids
So they made a contract wi' the Lord
To leave the pipe on Sunday
For a double score the night before
Would see them through till Monday

Loons is loons...

COLEBURN

IN 1897, A FIRM of Dundee whisky blenders (John Robertson and Son Ltd) constructed a distillery on a farm between Hart Hill and Brown Muir, just on the north side of the watershed on the road between Elgin and Rothes. The farm was called Coleburn, probably from an association with the activity of charcoal manufacture in the vicinity, and that became the name of the distillery. Water from the Glen Burn and a railway running through made it a good location for whisky-making. The architect was the ubiquitous Charles Cree Doig.

In 1916, Coleburn was sold to the Clynelish Distillery Co Ltd, which in 1930 became part of the SMD/DCL empire. It was finally put to sleep in 1985, at a time when distilleries were closing all over the place. For more or less 88 years it had worked quietly away making whisky for blenders, in the early days for Yellow Label, then for Usher's blends and more recently for Johnnie Walker Red. There have been few independent bottling, so Coleburn is rarely encountered as a single malt. I had a chance to try some at the Wild Whisky Weekend in Nykøbing, Falster, in Denmark in 2005 and it was a very decent dram.

There seems to be little of note in the history of Coleburn, though it did pioneer some advances in effluent purification. Somewhat ironically, effluent disposal seems to be an issue that haunts Coleburn. Charles Doig apparently lost eighteen months in the construction of Coleburn because of difficulties in providing a lavatory for the Excise Office. I shall refrain from speculating about why a toilet for Excise Officers might have been problematic.

UDV submitted an application to Moray Council in 1996 to convert the B-listed building into residential accommodation. The application was narrowly approved in principle but various difficulties, including sewage disposal, prevented the development from actually taking place. Diageo sold the site around 2004 to Dale and Mark Winchester, who have plans to develop it into a music village (with a concert space for 1,500 people), restaurant and hotel. They have to deal with the same planning issues, though realisation of this project does now seem likely.

The distilling plant has been dismantled, so the chances of Coleburn working again as a distillery are almost nil, but it is an attractive building, especially the lofty kiln with its pagoda roof, and will hopefully be developed in a way that preserves the dignity and honour of this distilling workhorse.

SCOTCH DRINK (Extract)

Robert Burns

Oh whisky! soul o' plays an pranks!
Accept a Bardie's gratefu thanks!
When wanting thee, what tuneless cranks
Are my poor verses!
Thou comes – they rattle I' their ranks,
At ither's arses.

FORSYTHS COPPERSMITHS

ONE OF THE THINGS that is least understood in the study of whisky distillation is the role of copper. Copper is a traditional material for whisky makers, though probably the early distillers preferred it mainly for its malleability; it was easy to work with and could be fashioned into the odd shapes required in swan necks and worm tubes. It also has excellent heat transfer properties. However, it actually plays an even more valuable role than that because it has a catalytic effect that removes sulphur from the distillate and thus cleans the spirit.

This effect may have been intuitively appreciated by some of the early expert whisky makers, but it has only really become obvious since some distillers tried to do away with copper in favour of other materials, especially stainless steel. Both in malt whisky and in grain whisky production, stainless steel was tried and found wanting. It has a neutral effect on the sulphur, which therefore stays in the whisky and means that it does not taste good. Aromas can be pungent, meaty, eggy and cabbagey — not really what you want in a whisky. Once copper has done its job, it cleans the spirit, leaving sweet, clean, fresh notes.

Allied Distillers tried stainless steel in still bottoms and condensers at Tormore and quickly had the copper put back. Grain distilleries experimented with stainless steel and found that in a column still there is an obvious advantage, in terms of structural strength and durability, but many had to put sacrificial copper into the stills to do the job that stainless steel cannot. Dailuaine is the only place in Speyside where I have seen stainless steel (in two of their condensers).

Most of the sulphur comes from the grain itself, and possibly from time to time from bacterial infection or the yeast. Some distillers look for a meaty, sulphury character in their new-makes, for what it can contribute to blends, but most are primarily interested in removing sulphur.

The key is in the degree of reflux in the distillation process. With reflux, the vapours of alcohol rise as steam but find their progress upwards difficult and fall back, requiring to rise again. The more reflux, the more contact there is between the copper and the spirit. Tall stills, stills with boil balls or lamp glass shapes, stills with ascending lyne arms, stills with purifiers; all these assist and promote reflux and so help produce a finer, cleaner whisky. Direct-fired stills have copper chain rummagers, which ensure a further degree of interplay between copper and spirit. Cooling is also an important part of the process, for the spirit has varying degrees of contact with the copper, depending on the form – more with shell and tube condensers and less with worm tubs.

Constructing, repairing and replacing worn parts of these stills and condensers is the job of the coppersmith. William Grant's have their own coppersmith, but the two main players in Scotland are Abercrombie's of Alloa, who are now owned by Diageo, and Forsyths of Rothes, who are independent. A visit to the Forsyths yard in Rothes is an interesting experience; parts of stills lie around the workshop floor or in the yard outside, striking the eye incongruously, like half-made bridges or dismembered body parts. Benches are covered in interesting tools and sheets of copper and heaps of copper wire rings lie on the ground, destined to become rummagers (fewer of these now that less stills are direct-fired). The noise of cutting, abrading and hammering can be deafening.

As far back as the early 18th century, there was a Morayshire Copper and Brass Works in Rothes, owned by a Robert Baillie. Baillie sold the business to Robert Willison, who already had yards in Alloa and Sunderland. Willison wanted to retire in 1933 and, as he had no sons or other family members who wished to assume control of the business, he sold the three yards separately to their managers. The Alloa business was sold to R. G. Abercrombie and the Rothes plant was purchased by Alex Forsyth.

Alex's son Ernest also joined the business, though he was away in the army during the Second World War. Ernest, known as 'Toot', learned a great deal about welding in the army and, on his return to Rothes after the war, started experimenting with welding stills instead of riveting them. Some distillers were concerned about this as distillers tend to have a natural conservatism that is reluctant to mess with still design in any way. One of them was quite dismissive, saying 'a still without rivets is like a naked lady'. 'Well, what's wrong with that?' thought Toot.

The present managing director is Richard Forsyth, grandson of Alex Forsyth. He is an affable man who was happy to show me around and not just answer my questions but also regale me with stories over a dram. I learned a lot about the history of Forsyths and their activities, not just in Speyside and Scotland but also overseas, as they have been involved in (mainly distilling) projects on every continent. I learned about how they took over the only local rival, Grants of Dufftown, in 1981. The plumbing and electrical part of Grants, though owned by Forsyths, is still called Grants. I learned about the programme of diversification that has resulted in them working for offshore oil, paper and pharmaceutical industries. Distilling remains, however, their core business.

I asked Richard to tell me the kind of problems that coppersmiths have to deal with in the whisky industry. One of the main issues is access, as old still-houses were not designed to make it easy to get stills in and out. That is less true of some of the newer distilleries, where access can be much more straightforward. In the old days, stills were put into existing buildings and ease of access was someone else's problem. This means that fairly frequently, walls have to be dismantled or roofs lifted to remove and replace whole stills. Sometimes it is easier to build the still *in situ*, though that takes much longer and can impact on production.

Responding to emergencies is also something that happens less often these days. It seems that in the past, distillers were more likely to work their stills past the point where they should have been checked and patched. Stills would become too thin (Richard has seen stills pulsating because of this) and could burst or, with the vacuum effect, crumple like a paper bag. Stills were also more likely to be burnt on the bottom, like a pot left too long on the stove. Technological improvements, training and health and safety requirements have all helped to improve this situation.

Different parts of different still types wear at different rates. Richard told me that in wash stills, the neck, lyne arm and condensers can need to be replaced after eight years, whereas the shoulder and pot can go on for 20 or 25 years. In spirit stills it is the shoulder and the body that might need replaced after eight to 12 years, while the necks and condensers can

last for 30 years. Rummagers wear the copper inside stills more quickly, but then the relevant parts are normally constructed out of much thicker copper to cope with that, which may impact on cost but negates the impact on the speed of wear.

What happens to all that copper wearing out inside a still? Does it end up in the whisky? Apparently not, according to Richard, though it does end up in the pot ale and spent lees. Much of this is applied directly to fields, which, as the agricultural land around Speyside tends to be copper-deficient, means that farmers no longer have to drive to Elgin to buy copper-rich fertiliser. If small amounts also end up in the feed of cattle, there's no great problem because farmers would probably buy copper and zinc supplements anyhow (though too much copper is not good for sheep). So, all in all, it seems quite a nicely balanced, benign cycle, with copper being the all-round good guy.

GALWAY CITY (Extract)

*Did you ever see the grass in the morning all
  bedecked with jewels rare?*
*Did you ever see a handsome lassie, diamonds
  sparkling in her hair?*
*Did you ever see a copper kettle mended with
  an ould tin can?*
*Did you ever see a handsome lassie married
  off to an ugly man?*

GLEN GRANT

THE TOWN OF ROTHES sits by a bend in the Spey at a point where the river runs off in a north-easterly direction towards Fochabers and eventually the sea, while the main road to Elgin veers off to the north west. Barnard said of the town, 'For beauty of position nothing that we have seen can excel the situation of Rothes.' That is still true today. The town and the river valley are dominated by the forest-clad slopes of Ben Aigan two miles to the west, and Ben Rinnes can also be seen in the east. None of the Rothes distilleries are particularly visible to anyone driving through the town but unfortunately the dark grains plant is, constantly belching several plumes of thick cloud into the atmosphere like something from the nasty end of a tale by Tolkien.

Glen Grant, named after the founding family rather than a place, is the biggest and the oldest of the town's four distilleries and produces the third best selling malt in the world. It was founded in 1840 by brothers John and James Grant, who cut their whisky teeth by managing Aberlour distillery for eight years. These brothers were a real pair of Victorian characters. James, in particular, had a huge reputation in the area. He trained as a lawyer and eventually got into banking. He was provost of Elgin for 15 years from 1848 to 1863 and was a passionate activist in favour of bringing the railways into the North East. He was largely responsible for the development of the Morayshire rail network, which reached Rothes in 1858. The town declared a public holiday in celebration.

James Grant's son (also called James) took over the business in 1872. Known as the Major, he was also a flamboyant figure. He built Glen Grant house and its extensive gardens, which are still an attractive bonus to visitors. The Major was a keen sportsman, enjoyed fishing and hunting, created a curling pond in the town and was the first man in the Highlands to own a car. He also visited Africa and India, indulging his passion for big game hunting. There is a 'dram hut' in the gardens which has a definite African style.

On one of his trips to Africa, the Major found a Matabele boy by the side of the road. The boy seemed to have been orphaned, perhaps by some tribal conflict, and abandoned. The Major brought him home to Rothes, where he was looked after by the family and later employed as their butler, and where he lived until he passed away at the age of 85 in 1972. Biawa (pronounced 'byeway') Makalaga played for Rothes football team in the 1920s. His gravestone is in the churchyard overlooking Glenrothes distillery, where his ghost has apparently been seen. Richard Forsyth told me that one of Biaiwa's favourite sayings was 'Loons is loons the warld roond but Rothes loons is buggers!'

The Major died in 1931 and control of the distillery passed to his grandson, Douglas Mackessack, who also became known as the Major. Described as 'one of the last of the old gentleman distillers', he became a very popular figure in the community of Rothes and among the workforce at the distillery. It was thanks to Douglas Mackessack that Glen Grant became such a force in Italy. In the early 1960s, Armando Giovinetti came to Scotland on a pilgrimage to the land of single malt. He wanted to try selling the stuff in his home country and Mackessack was one of the few, if not the only distiller, who gave Armando his trust and 50 cases of whisky. That trust was rewarded as Giovinetti did a remarkable job in introducing malt whisky to the Italians.

Glen Grant distillery started off on a fairly small scale; in the beginning, all motive power was provided by a water wheel. As it expanded, however, steam engines were brought in. Barnard was impressed by the 'two fine engines' and the fact that the distillery had electric lighting, 'the first time in any manufacturing place in the North of Scotland'. Barnard saw the usual 'large stacks of peat' and also 'stacks of ice, for summer use, covered with sawdust and thatched with straw.'

JAMES GRANT JNR · 1872

Barnard was impressed by the purifiers he saw above the stills. These purifiers (still working today) were pioneered by the Grants in an attempt to provide finer whisky. According to a 19th century promotional leaflet, 'Glen Grant is pure, mild and agreeable; the essential oils and impurities, which render other Whiskies harsh and disagreeable, are, in the GLEN-GRANT WHISKEY, detected and separated from it in the process of manufacture.' A handy thing to be able to claim at a time (1872) when the adulterated whisky scandal in Glasgow was all over the newspapers. Other innovations at Glen Grant include the drum maltings, which, in 1888, were the first to be installed at any distillery in Scotland, and which survived until 1971.

After two years of operation, Glen Grant was producing about 40,000 gallons a year. By the time Barnard came to call, this had gone up to 234,000 gallons. A few years after Barnard's visit, Glen Grant was so in need of expansion that the Major built Glen Grant No 2 (later Caperdonich) just across the road. Nonetheless, Glen Grant No 1 continued to grow and there have been various expansions over the years, as well as changes to the production practices. Barnard saw four stills and now there are eight. Previously, one wash still and one spirit still were of a smaller size, the small spirit still being affectionately known as 'Wee Geordie' after a fireman who reckoned it made the best spirit. The small stills were replaced with larger ones in 1987 and 'Wee Geordie' now stands outside the distillery office.

The present scale of production at Glen Grant is impressive. The mash tun takes 59,000 litres. Ten large washbacks of Oregon pine hold 19,000 litres each and the eight tall stills together produce approximately 5.5 million litres of spirit a year. The stills are described by the distillery workers as 'mushrooms and onions' in reference to their shape, though others have said the wash stills have a German helmet shape. However you describe it, the shape is unique to Glen Grant. The considerable production is carried out by five men.

Very little of the output at Glen Grant is used for blending. The market soaks up the single malt quite readily and there is very little spare. The standard, no-age-statement Glen Grant is the top selling malt in Italy and third in the world. It is aged mainly in bourbon casks, whereas sherry wood is favoured for the 10 year old. There is also a 14 year old cask strength expression not readily available in the shops; though in truth very little Glen Grant gets into UK shops at all.

I was guided round and given samples by a tour guide called Alice, a woman of considerable character and accent ('Hope ye enjoyed yur toor of Glen Grunt!'). The younger whisky is quite pale (all have natural colour) and fresh. The 10 year old is maltier and sweeter, with a definite nutty character which becomes nutmeg spice with water. The best time to visit would be in the summer, when one might enjoy some of the lovely whisky in the surroundings of the distillery gardens, which are its natural home.

When Pernod Ricard took over Allied Domecq in 2005, they had to get rid of Glen Grant. It was eventually bought by Campari, so the historic connection between Glen Grant and Italy has now had a new boost. A feeling of greater optimism, confidence and ambition is being promoted by the new owners.

HERE'S TO YOU AGAIN (Extract)

Alexander Rodger

Your wine it may do for the bodies far south,
But a Scotsman likes something that bites i'
*   the mouth,*
And whisky's the thing that can do't to a tee.
Then Scotsmen and whisky will ever agree;
For wi' toddlin' but and toddlin' ben,
Sae lang we've been nurst on't we hardly
*   can spean.*

GLEN SPEY

WHEN BARNARD VISITED Glen Spey, he declared it to be 'the newest distillery in the district'. Originally it had been a meal mill, the Mill of Rothes, but around 1884/85 it was turned into a distillery by the owner, James Stuart, a corn merchant who was involved with both Macallan and Glenrothes distilleries. Very shortly after Barnard's visit, Stuart sold the distillery to the famous wine and gin merchants W & A Gilbey. This was the first time an English company had bought a Scottish malt distillery.

Barnard does not have much to say about Glen Spey, despite its modernity. The maltings that he mentions were removed in 1969, at the time when J&B modernised and doubled the capacity of the distillery. Over the years, Glen Spey has pioneered a few technologies. It was the first to install a semi-lauter mash tun, and this style actually became known as the 'Glen Spey tun'. The Glen Spey stills, which seemed a very dark copper colour to me, operate at 4psi, which is half the pressure of most stills, and their internal heating arrangement involves radiators rather than coils or kettles. They are a decent size, with restricted waists and lamp glass shape, and have purifiers (which I did not see as they are outside the stillroom), for achieving extra reflux.

The spirit from Glen Spey is therefore light, elegant, floral and smooth. It is only really available as a single malt in the Flora and Fauna range, though it turns up from time to time in independent bottlings. It contributes to J&B, and in particular to Spey Royal. There is a very ancient bottle of Castle Glen Spey, bottled by W & A Gilbey, in the distillery office. The bottle, which is two-thirds full, has a picture on the label of 'Glen Spey Glenlivet Distillery' and a certification that they produce 'over two and a half million bottles of whisky annually'. Gilbeys sold up in 1962 and the distillery capacity was doubled in 1970 to stand at around two million litres, so the claim seems unlikely. Sadly, the cloudy, discoloured liquid looks like it would be no longer drinkable.

Glen Spey has had its share of unfortunate events. In 1892 a particularly heavy snowfall collapsed the roof of an elegant iron-span warehouse. There is no record of whether any stocks were lost or if it simply chilled the whisky. In 1920 the distillery suffered a fire, though the warehouses were saved. During the Second World War, Glen Spey was used as a billet for soldiers and it seems that one of them was electrocuted in an accident. A number of people have reported seeing his ghost. On the day when I visited Glen Spey the distillery had been silent for a few months and was still and deserted. As I was shown into the fermentation room, with its eight stainless steel washbacks, I heard some strange fluttering, bumping noises coming from somewhere. I put it down to birds on the roof or behind a wall and left quickly, without investigating further.

Barnard makes reference to the fact that Glen Spey lies 'just underneath the hill on which stands the ruins of the Castle of Rothes, the ancient seat of the noble family of Leslies, Earls of Rothes.' There is little left of the castle now, but it was an imposing fortress in its day. It is very close to the distillery and looms above it, so that it must surely have always overshadowed it, even back in the days when it was the Mill of Rothes. The castle is a very ancient one. It was built around 1200 by Petrus de Pollack. The Pollack family had been brought there by King William the Lion in the 1160s, to bring stability to a lawless area. The castle was four storeys high and protected by a natural drop on three sides and a dry moat with a drawbridge and portcullis on the fourth. It would have had a commanding position and good views of the surrounding area.

Edward I, the Hammer of the Scots, stayed at Rothes Castle on his northern campaign in 1296, the guest of Norman Leslie. The Leslie family held the castle for nearly 400 years. It was burned by local people in 1662 to prevent it being used as a den by thieves. The present town of Rothes really dates from 1766, when the Earl of Seafield, who owned the estate, set out a crofting township. Apparently much of the stone of the ruined castle was used to build the crofts, which explains why so little of it remains.

DYNASTIC SHENANIGANS

Sir George Leslie, son of Norman Leslie, was described as 'Dominus de Rothes' in 1392. He was an influential man and was granted the Barony of Fythkill in Fife (later called Leslie) by the sovereign in 1398, for the annual rent of a pair of gloves.

His grandson, also George Leslie, became the first Earl of Rothes. He married three times and it seems that when he grew tired of his second wife he obtained a divorce on the grounds that they were in fact related and thus the marriage was null and void. Unfortunately his eldest son had by that time married into the powerful St Clair family and it would not have gone well with them if he had been declared illegitimate, so George Leslie got a special ruling protecting his children's rights on the basis that he only found out about the incestuous nature of his marriage after they were born.

The grandson of the first earl, another George, became the second earl. He was described as a ne'er-do-well and was outlawed for his part in a murder. He was a spendthrift and mismanaged the family affairs so badly that his brother William appealed to King James IV in 1506 and got approval for a family council to take over the management of the estate.

William, indeed, became the third Earl of Rothes but was unfortunately killed, soon after, at the Battle of Flodden.

The fourth earl was his son, George. He was an able nobleman and was appointed ambassador to Denmark in 1550. In 1558, he was one of eight commissioners elected to represent Scotland at the marriage of Queen Mary to the Dauphin of France. He died mysteriously at Dieppe on his way home, along with the Earl of Cassillis and Bishop Reid, president of the court of session. Lord Fleming died about the same time at Paris and it was believed that they had all been poisoned because they refused to settle on the Dauphin the crown matrimonial of Scotland. George was married five times.

His oldest son, Norman, was passed over for inheritance due to his treasonable involvement in the murder of Cardinal Beaton. Norman ended up in France, fighting in the service of the French king. He was mortally wounded at the battle of Cambray in 1554, though his gallantry and bravery in battle were widely acclaimed.

The fifth earl, Andrew, was also involved in the affairs of Mary of Guise and her daughter, Mary Queen of Scots. He fought for Mary's cause at the battle of Langside.

His grandson, John, became the sixth earl. He was a passionate Covenanter who went to London in 1640 with other commissioners, to discuss their objections with the king. He appears to have become seduced by the pomp, wealth and power of the London court and was won over by the king's arguments. He was to have stayed in London with a royal pension, married to the daughter of an English noble family, but he died at Richmond, aged 41.

In 1647, in one of the most notorious events of the Civil War, an evil deed was perpetrated by the Covenanters, under General David Leslie. They had been pursuing a defeated Royalist army down the length of the Kintyre peninsula. At Dunaverty Castle, on the southernmost tip of the peninsula, the Royalists knew they had reached the end of the line. Though they surrendered to General Leslie, the Covenanters massacred all 300 of them in cold blood. The locals still refer to Dunaverty as 'Blood Rock'.

John, the seventh earl, was a Royalist who was taken prisoner at the Battle of Worcester. At the restoration of Charles II, he was given a pension and high office, and became the Duke of Rothes. Unfortunately, he was seriously prone to licentious and debauched behaviour, ending up permanently either sick or drunk. The dukedom ended when he died in 1661.

In 1711 John, ninth Earl of Rothes, sold the Rothes estate to John Grant of Elchies. It now belongs to the Earl of Seafield. When John sold the estate, he 'reserved to himself the castle tower, with the castle bank and the green under the walls thereof', the only remnant of the vast estates which the Rothes family at one time possessed in Morayshire.

GLENROTHES

GLENROTHES WAS THE second distillery to be built in the town of Rothes. It was constructed in 1878 on the site of an old sawmill by the Burn of Rothes, which carries pure water from high on the Mannoch Hills, running in classic form over granite and through peat. The distillery also uses spring water from the Ardcanny and Branchhill springs and from the Fairies Well (the legendary site of a double murder in the late fourteenth century, when Margaret, daughter of Norman Leslie, and her lover were assassinated by a henchman of Alexander Stewart, the Wolf of Badenoch). Production commenced on 28 December 1879, and the first spirit run came on the same stormy night that the Tay Bridge collapsed and a passenger train fell into the icy waters below.

When Barnard visited Glenrothes, the motive power for the entire distillery was provided by the Burn of Rothes, including grain elevators, pumps and 'a revolving stirring-gear' in the mash tun. Barnard seems to have been impressed by the layout of the distillery and the fact that cement and concrete were much in evidence; 'a huge Worm Tub [had] been erected, constructed with cement, a favourite material of this establishment' and the still-house had a 'concreted floor, daily deluged with water'. The distillery itself was built in stone but the five warehouses were constructed of concrete. Barnard does not tell us what the roofs were made of, but 10 years later one collapsed under the weight of snow.

The 'large stock of Peats in the sheds' and the 'capital Cooperage', along with all that flammable spirit, give some explanation for Barnard's comment that 'the arrangements for extinguishing fire consist of fire plugs, hose, and extincteurs.' Unfortunately, these arrangements were found wanting in 1922, when one warehouse was destroyed by fire and 200,000 gallons of whisky exploded, leading to 'a stream of burning whisky' running into the Burn of Rothes. It is said that not only were local anglers easily able to catch the drunken trout, but that they required no further cooking. Part of the distillery was again destroyed by fire in 1962.

Barnard, as usual, reserves his most poetic language for the scenery and the landscape that he witnessed on his leisurely journey to the distillery. He is perhaps worth quoting in full:

When our train neared Rothes, the beauties of the valley became more apparent than on the previous day, as the atmosphere was clearer. Our eyes were enchanted by the picturesque and smiling grandeur of the valley; the steep wooded hills provided one vast expanse of foliage of various shades and tints, and scarcely a barren spot or boulder was visible on the mountain side to mar the peaceful aspect of the scene; while the Spey, the most rapid and capricious of all the rivers in Scotland, ploughed its way between cliffs of gravel and rocks, the sides of which were arrayed in a robe of greenery and the haughs above covered with trembling birches.

That beauty is still there, but sadly no longer to be viewed from a passing train.

Glenrothes was originally founded under the direction of James Stuart (owner of Macallan). But in the first few months one of the financial backers, the City of Glasgow Bank, collapsed and Stuart left to build Glen Spey next door, leaving the remaining partners to complete the distillery on a smaller scale than originally intended. One of these partners was Robert Dick, who was resident partner at the time of Barnard's visit. Soon afterwards, in 1887, the company amal-

gamated with Bunnahabhain and formed Highland Distillers Ltd.

When Barnard visited, Glenrothes had two stills and a potential capacity of approximately 600,000 litres. In the 1890s, the distillery was doubled in size and the output recorded at 1.2 million litres. A further two stills were added in 1963, and in 1979 the still-house was completely rebuilt. Total output is now very nearly six million litres per annum,

making it one of the biggest malt distilleries in Scotland. The 1979 still-house is known as the Cathedral, for very good reasons. It is quite a stunning place to visit, with its five wash stills and five spirit stills ranked on either side of a central isle, with rows of condensers in between; a copper cathedral indeed.

Glenrothes stills are only filled to three-fifths of capacity and the distillation is a leisurely 12 hours. This, combined with the boil ball still shape and the condensers, leads to a greater exposure to copper and therefore a lighter, more refined spirit. In addition the regime is slightly unusual in allowing the stills to rest for 12 hours in between charges. This, it is believed, increases the patina and allows the copper to reoxidise, all to the benefit of the final spirit.

Fermentation takes place over 52 hours at Glenrothes, which has eight stainless steel washbacks and 12 wooden ones. John Sutherland, the distillery manger, says he has a slight preference for wood, though he doubts that there is much significant difference. Wood may harbour some flora and fauna in its cracks and crevices and that may add to the flavour, though the days of cleaning with heather besoms is over and a steam clean at 130° will zap most of those. Stainless steel washbacks on the other hand are easier to clean and have a much longer life. Glenrothes has not yet tried separate distillations to find out whether there is any significant difference in spirit character. Some companies in the wine industry have reverted to wood after trying stainless steel but I have not heard of this happening in any distillery.

Glenrothes still belongs to the same company that built it (the parent company is now the Edrington Group) but the single malt expressions are managed and sold (under license) by Berry Bros and Rudd, who have had a long and positive relationship with the owners over 74 years, mainly through their buying single malt whisky for their very successful Cutty Sark blend. In 1991, Highland invited Berry Bros and Rudd to take on sales of a single malt from one of their distilleries. After examining a few, Berry Bros and Rudd chose Glenrothes and found it to be a distillery with great promise and potential, including some very interesting stocks. Glenrothes, one of the three most popular malts in Scotland among blenders, had not previously been bottled as a single malt – a real hidden treasure.

To begin with, Berry Bros produced a 12 year old expression, but they quickly realised that they would do better to bring their 300 years' experience of selling fine wines to bear on the product. They considered the stocks and began a series of vintage expressions of the Glenrothes, which by their very nature are limited editions. The presentation, in dumpy bottles and hand-written labels, which remind one of sample bottles, bound in cardboard, with a fixing disc to secure the base, is unique and attractive.

For my visit to Glenrothes, I was picked up in Dufftown by Ronnie Cox, a director of Berry Bros and Rudd, and Marcin Miller, in a Renault Cabriolet with the roof down. I had to sit in the back for the eight mile ride: a real turbo-charged experience!

In one of the warehouses, we were joined by distillery manager, John Sutherland, and three other guests, and we had the amusing experience of drawing our own valinch samples from a number of casks to explore and discover the impact of different casks at different ages. Later, in Rothes House (the old Manse, owned by Berry Bros and Rudd), we had a group tasting of the Glenrothes new-make and five of the vintage expressions. These vintages are not single casks, but vattings of different woods from a given year. Some of these are very likely to become collectable.

Because Berry Bros and Rudd have gone down this limited-edition, vintage-single-malt road, the whiskies in the range are all different. This one tastes of liquorice and sherbet while the next one is honey, orange and chocolate; one is a coy ballerina, the next an in-your-face pole dancer. What they all have in common is quality, exquisite balance, subtlety and sophistication; carefully made whisky from cleverly selected casks.

As if that were not enough of a treat, in the evening we were treated to a 'Cutty Sark International Dinner', with more vintage whiskies partnering excellent dishes, including chicken consommé with quails' eggs and devils on horseback; a most memorable evening of the finest hospitality. Pleasant dreams were already beginning to swirl in the taxi on the way home.

BIAWA'S GHOST

After the 1979 rebuild of the still-house, one of the new stills (No 4) was giving trouble and its performance was not conforming to expectations or to the other stills. At the same time, at least two of the stillmen had reported being aware of a 'presence' or ghost in the still-house on -occasions when they were working alone there on winter nights. In appearance, the ghost was unmistakably that of a well-known Rothes character, Biawa Makalaga, who had died in 1972. Biawa had been the butler to Major James Grant, and his story is told under the entry for Glen Grant distillery.

Some of the workers had mentioned this to Paul Rickards, head of spirit quality with Robertson and Baxter. Paul had known Biawa since 1962. He also knew Professor Cedric Wilson, a pharmacologist who had developed a deep professional interest in the paranormal. Approval was obtained from head office to arrange a visit to the distillery by Cedric Wilson. Professor Wilson surveyed the site using a dowsing technique and quickly concluded that a ley line had been damaged by the construction of the new still-house.

Ley lines are lines of earth energy, disputed by many scientists but recognised by those who consider that science gives us only a partial understanding of the world. They were certainly important to ancient peoples. Cedric Wilson ordered two stakes of pig iron from the company engineers and these were sunk into the ground on either side of the still-house. This 'repaired' the ley line, allowing the flow of earth energy to be resumed. Paul Rickards says that 'a silence descended on the place as the previously unnoticed tension was relieved.'

Even more curiously, Cedric sat in the still-house for about 20 minutes to try to establish contact with the ghost. He had not been told of the whereabouts of Biawa's grave but suddenly strode decisively up through the cemetery, until he stood by the very gravestone. After some 10 minutes he returned to the group and declared that his mission had been accomplished and that the earthbound spirit had accepted his need to depart. The ghost has never since been seen and, as far as I can tell, still No 4 now operates perfectly well.

Thanks to Paul Rickards for the story.

CUTTY SARK

Cutty Sark was launched by Berry Bros and Rudd in 1923. The label was designed by the artist James McBey. It was never meant to be a bright yellow label but a printer's error resulted in something that the company preferred to the label that had been intended. The blend Cutty Sark was named after the tea clipper Cutty Sark, which was the fastest clipper ever built. That in turn was named after the young scantily clad witch in Robert Burns' poem 'Tam o' Shanter'. She was the fastest of all the witches that chased Tam that night, and managed to pull the tail from his horse before he could reach the safety of the bridge.

It is not clear whether Berry Bros and Rudd realised they were naming their whisky after a young witch with strong legs and a bare bum, but there is an interesting coming together of earthly and unearthly spirits in 'Tam o' Shanter', just as there is in the story of Cedric Wilson's visit to Glenrothes.

SPEYBURN

THESE DAYS, to visit Speyburn distillery you take the Mosstodloch road out of Rothes and the entrance is tucked away on the left hand side, just as you are leaving the town. The distillery seems squeezed in on one side of a beautiful glen, through which runs the Granty Burn. The nearby hill is called Cnock na Croiche, which translates 'Hillock of the Gibbet'. Here, in the old days, criminals were dispatched at the end of a rope. Local people often refer to Speyburn as 'the gibbet'. Speyburn also sat next to the Elgin to Craigellachie railway, though it was not directly connected and always sent its precious cargo by road to Rothes Station. This idyllic glen is now haunted by spectral trains as well as the tormented souls of brutally executed criminals.

The distillery was built in 1897 by brothers John and Edward Hopkins (John Hopkins & Co also owned Tobermory distillery at that time). Apparently built of stones taken from the former bed of the River Spey, it was designed by Charles Doig, who made the best use he could of a cramped site by designing the distillery on three floors. Applying the same principles that drove New York to develop skyscrapers forced Doig to adopt some interesting technologies, especially in the maltings.

1897 was the year of Queen Victoria's diamond jubilee and Hopkins was very keen that some whisky should be distilled with 1897 as its date of production. However, delays in construction meant that production could only begin in the last week of December. With no doors or windows in place and a howling blizzard making conditions very uncomfortable, the distillery managed to fill and bond one single butt of spirit in the year 1897. It would be interesting to know what happened to that butt.

When I visited Speyburn, the distillery had just undergone a programme of renewal and automation. The signs of change were there — a gleaming new Hamworthy gas boiler, shiny new malt bins (the mark of the recently removed wooden bins was still to be painted over) and various other things that Bobby Anderson proudly showed me: smart control panels and a state-of-the-art system that recovers heat from spent lees, pot ale and the hot water leaving the worm tubs, in order to pre-heat the charge going into the still. This may be the first of its kind.

However, I suspect that Bobby was also proud of some of the older remnants in Speyburn too. Good whisky men can appreciate the old and the new at the same time. This was the first malt distillery in Scotland to install pneumatic drum maltings. In 1897, when Speyburn was built, these Hennings drums were a cutting-edge piece of kit allowing a greater capacity in less space, with fewer workers and the ability to operate all year round. The malt started off in the loft storage on the third floor and descended one level to the steeps. The three steeps then supplied malt to six drums. These were rotated slowly and humidified air was passed through to achieve the right conditions for the malt to germinate.

When first installed, the drums were driven by a 12 horse power steam engine, though electric power took over in the 1940s. They stopped working in 1967 and stand now, complete with belt drives and conveyors, as silent milestones on the road of progress in whisky-making. The building that contains them is grade 2 listed. The distillery is also unusual in having two kiln floors, one above the other. This

made best use of the space and was energy efficient, allowing the top floor of green malt to be pre-dried before dropping down to the lower level. The original Doig pagoda is still in place.

Speyburn also retains a wooden spirit receiver and six fine washbacks made of Douglas fir and about 50 years old. The Boby mill dates from around 1925, although the malt intake and milling is now computerised by PLC (Programmable Logic Controllers). The mash tun has old-fashioned rake and arm stirring gear and in the still-house, the operator can see what is happening through the viewing port in the still neck by means of an old dressing table mirror strapped to a beam. It doesn't have to be pretty, as long

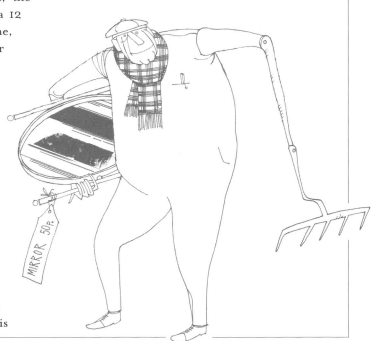

as it works. Speyburn still uses worm tubs, believing that the positive effect on the spirit outweighs the expense of having to replace all that copper on a regular basis. However, the tanks were changed from wood to stainless steel in 1993.

Speyburn distillery passed from the hands of John Hopkins & Co in 1916 when it was bought over by DCL. It was sold to Inver House Distillers in January 1992. This distillery encapsulates the march of engineering progress, with fascinating snapshots from different periods of the ever-advancing technology. The story of whisky distillation, like that of most industries, is a perpetual compromise between the old and the new.

The spirit has nutty and spicy characteristics. These translate through into the proprietary 10 year old expression, with its nose of nuts, putty and cinnamon, developing tobacco and melon. Various independent bottlings are also available; the Gordon and MacPhail 1974 bottling is particularly good. Most Speyburn, however, finds its way into blends, including those of its previous owners, Diageo.

ADDRESS TO THE BARLEY SEED (Extract)

Anon

*When the Lord first planted oot the earth
wi' trees an' flo'ers an' weeds,
He scattered roon' Speyside a puckle barley
seeds;
Thus was the birth o' Scotia's brew on that
fair springtime morn,
For in the month that followed, John
Barleycorn was born.*

CHARLESTOWN OF ABERLOUR

Upriver from Rothes we find the village of Craigellachie
and the town of Aberlour. Here the River Fiddich flows between
the hills of Ben Aigan and Ben Rinnes to join the Spey.
This is the true heart of Speyside whisky country.
Craigellachie has long been a crossroads, a place where railways,
roads and rivers meet. Aberlour, once famous for its orphanage,
is the home of Walkers Shortbread.

ABERLOUR
BENRINNES
CRAIGELLACHIE
GLENALLACHIE
THE MACALLAN
THE SPEYSIDE COOPERAGE

Photo: John Dewar & Sons Ltd

ABERLOUR

WHERE THE PAST LINGERS IN THE PRESENT

Barnard had nice things to say about Aberlour: a 'perfect model distillery' in a 'charming village'. Aberlour was still a young town when Barnard visited. It had become a burgh in 1814 and was named Charlestown of Aberlour after Charles Grant of Wester Elchies. He was the laird whose vision transformed Aberlour from a sleepy village to a bustling town with grid pattern, nice broad High Street and town square. Thomas Telford's Craigellachie Bridge also dates from 1814. It must have been a time of new beginnings and optimism in Aberlour.

It is still a charming place with attractive gardens (the Alice Littler Park), interesting shops (including the delightful Spey Larder deli), cafés, restaurants and bars (the Mash Tun, in particular, stands for that great trilogy of whisky, good food and hospitality). Aberlour, of course, is also the home of Aberlour distillery. Helen Gardiner, tour guide at Cardhu distillery, comes from Aberlour. She told me that the town contains the aromatic essence of Speyside whisky, with the distillery at one end, the shortbread factory at the other and the floral displays in between.

A number of historical sites exist around Aberlour but the most interesting in the context of the distillery is St Drostan's Well. Drostan was supposed to have been a pupil or nephew of St Columba who came to Scotland as a missionary in the 6th century. He has a number of connections with various places in the North East, including Aberdour on the Buchan coast, which might be a source of confusion. But the legend that he baptised Pictish converts with water from a spring near where the Lour meets the Spey seems reasonable enough. That spring became known as St Drostan's Well, and the well-head stone is still preserved at the distillery.

The original Aberlour distillery, which dated from 1826, was established by James Gordon and Peter Weir. This was the distillery that the Grant brothers (of Glen Grant) managed during the 1830s. It was demolished in 1878, either because of a fire or to allow the construction of the Aberlour Preparatory School, or perhaps indeed for both reasons. The replacement distillery was constructed on a nearby site by James Fleming and commenced production in 1880. Fleming had a lease on the Mill of Ruthvie on the Lour and was manager of Dailuaine distillery. The new Aberlour was the realisation of his dream of owning his own distillery. He designed the layout himself.

Appropriately for the location and for a distillery designed by a mill owner, Fleming's plant was entirely run by water power. This arrangement impressed the reporter of the *Elgin Courant and Courier* when the distillery was opened. It also impressed Alfred Barnard when he visited the place just a few years later: 'There is no steam power in this distillery, the continuous flow of water being sufficient to drive all the machinery, which includes grinding, mashing, elevating, steering and pumping.' He was even impressed by the way the burn water was also used for cooling purposes, running over the worms and 'proving the simplest and most effectual condensing method we have met with.'

James Fleming made quite an impact on the town of Aberlour. He bequeathed it the Fleming Hall, the Cottage Hospital and the Suspension Bridge (he was moved to do so when a child was drowned after falling out of the ferry boat). Fleming sold the distillery in 1892 to Robert Thorne and Sons and died three years later. Barnard makes no mention of James Fleming.

Thorne immediately expanded the distillery and then, when a part of it was damaged by fire in 1898, completely rebuilt it, making it even bigger and better than before. The next substantial expansion took place in 1973, when S. Campbell & Sons doubled production. During that programme of work, a bottle of whisky and a newspaper were found secreted behind a particular stone. I believe another time capsule has now taken their place.

Nowadays, the things that are striking to the visitor are the stainless steel washbacks with their bright yellow coats of paint, the highly polished stills and, outside the main buildings, the whinstone towers. These were built in the 1930s to filter, clean and cool the waste water from the condensers before it ran back into the Lour. The towers are no longer in use at Aberlour, and I have never seen anything like them at any other distillery. The official tour of the distillery, available twice daily, is very thorough and finishes up in one of the warehouses, where visitors are treated to a tasting of five expressions of Aberlour and a sample of the new-make spirit. The new-make is very interesting, with sweetness nicely balanced by liquorice, pepper and spice.

Aberlour is one of a growing number of distilleries at which you can fill your own bottle from a cask at the visitor centre. I acquired two bottles of their nectar – one from a sherry cask and one from a cask of bourbon wood. The sherry cask whisky is deep mahogany colour, with a wonderful nose of raisins, toffee apples, pot pourri and Christmas cake. The taste is of oranges and Oddfellows spicy sweets; a very warming and delicious fireside dram, which I enjoyed towards the end of the year. It brought the smiling winter sun of Jerez into my heart. I am saving its bourbon sister for a special occasion.

Similar in style to the single sherry cask is the Aberlour a'bunadh. The Gaelic name means 'the origin', and it was created as a tribute to James Fleming. It is supposed to be the kind of dram that Fleming would have been familiar with. It therefore has to be from a sherry cask, full strength, with no caramel colouring, no chill-filtering and of no age statement. The small batch that was made in 1997 sold very quickly and the company had to make another. To date, about 17 batches have now appeared. A'bunadh, with its exotic spicy orange aromas

entwined with sumptuous Oloroso, is one of my favourite drams; it goes particularly well with good chocolate.

A'BUNADH AND CHOCOLATE LIMERICKS

Robin Laing

There was an old man from Corunna
Who ate chocolate dipped in a'bunadh
He said "This great thing
Has sweetened death's sting,
But I wish I'd discovered it sooner."

There once was a hot-air ballooner
Who dined on the deck of a schooner,
It ended in bliss,
With dark chocolate (Swiss)
And a wine glass filled with a'bunadh.

A lady from Tristan da Cunha
Went solar and stellar and lunar,
On board of a rocket
Made out of chocolate
And powered along by a'bunadh.

There once was a fellow named Spooner
Who fancied himself as a crooner
He sang a few bars
About bocolate chars
Which he ate with a bass of a'glunadh

When Carl Orff composed 'O Fortuna'
He was probably drunk on a'bunadh
But the chocolate bars
In ladies boudoir's,
Why, that's just a scandalous rumour.

A ninety year old honeymooner
Found his bride had a poor sense of humour
When he couldn't perform
She replaced poor old Norm
With a King Size Twix and a'bunadh.

BENRINNES

AT WHITEHOUSE FARM, just a wee bit upstream from Milltown of Edinvillie, Peter McKenzie established a farm distillery in 1826. Soon after, on 3 August 1829, the North East of Scotland experienced a devastating flood, which in Speyside became known as 'the Muckle Spate'. You can just about catch echoes of a biblical-scale cataclysm in retellings of the stories to this day. Although a summer flood, river levels rose from three feet to 17 feet almost overnight. Livestock and people were lost, bridges were swept away and buildings and structures were destroyed. Water funnelled off the vast sweep of Ben Rinnes and the Conval Hills into the various burns feeding into the Lour, which exploded with great force. Whatever the shape and size of McKenzie's 'Benrinnis' distillery, it was washed away completely in this churning onslaught.

The replacement Benrinnes distillery was built nearby at Lower Lyne of Ruthrie in 1835. This too was essentially constructed within farm buildings. The present-day distillery is in the same spot, though it surely looks nothing like it did in 1835. It remains, however, an upland distillery. To leave Aberlour and head towards Milltown of Edinvillie is to climb into the bosom of the mountain, leaving the valley world behind. When I visited, the distillery was on weekend shutdown and the whole place seemed in some enchanted spell of silence. That included Edinvillie, where I saw a sign that said 'Caution – Free Range Children'. The children must all have been indoors, perhaps peering through curtains until the stranger had gone. Afterwards, I drove further up the road, which climbs and climbs until it comes out through the pass of Glaick Harnes to join the B9009 near Allt a Bhainne distillery.

When Barnard visited Benrinnes, he was very impressed by the mountain scenery, though perhaps not in a completely favourable way. He talks about looking back down over the beauties of the valley and being 'almost sorry that we have so soon exchanged it for the mighty hills, with their apparel of gloom and shade. These sudden and great changes in Highland scenery are very exciting, and leave impressions on the mind not easily effaced.' He tells us the distillery is at 1,030 feet elevation. In that he is mistaken, for it is only about 700 feet up the slope of the mountain, whose summit is 2,755 feet (840 metres).

There is a fascinating sentence in Barnard's account of his visit to Benrinnes: 'We afterwards traversed this route in the depth of winter with the snow lying deeply on the ground, and marvelled at the vivid green of the fir trees in the valley, and the distances revealed by the clear cold atmosphere of the mountain heights.' Why did Barnard come back here in winter? Was he doing follow-up research? Did he have a social invitation to return? Certainly he was treated hospitably and dragged off to the office for a dram as soon as he got out of his 'dog-cart'.

As usual, Barnard's account is a fascinating snapshot of the distillery, which has had a chequered history and a number of incarnations. I have already mentioned the original version at Whitehouse Farm, washed away in an avenging torrent. After it was rebuilt, ownership passed to John Innes, and later to William Smith, who was bankrupted in 1864. From that year onwards, it was David Edward, and later his son Alexander, who ran Benrinnes. Alexander went on to build Aultmore and Craigellachie distilleries and to buy the one in Oban.

In 1881, a fire destroyed the spirit store, the threshing mill and some outbuildings. It could have been a lot worse, and David Edwards held a celebratory ball for his staff and the local people as a thank-you for their efforts in putting out the fire. In 1896, the company was not so lucky and a second fire damaged the distillery extensively. Once more the distillery rose from the ashes, and this time with the latest equipment. Already it was completely changed from the place Barnard saw, which was dependent on water power for driving pumps and other machinery.

By a cruel twist of fate, the great whisky slump following the crash of Pattison's came only three years later. Benrinnes' sole agent was F.W. Brickmann, another Leith based spirit merchant; Brickmann's business also collapsed in 1899. In 1905 the company reported growth and increase in profit despite the still depressed state of the whisky market, but by 1908 the directors had to write down the capital from £80,096 to £39,800. After many years of struggle, John Dewar & Sons Ltd took over Benrinnes in 1922 and the chain of ownership led from there to SMD, UDV and now Diageo.

The distillery was modernised in 1951, at which time the water wheel disappeared. Then it was completely rebuilt in 1955. In 1966, the number of stills was increased from three to six, obviously to increase output. In 1991, Benrinnes was one of the distilleries that pioneered the computerised automation of the mashing process. Today it is a very clean, bright, efficient-looking plant, though it clings to tradition in things like wooden washbacks and worm tubs for cooling the spirit runs.

The Benrinnes stills are worth some consideration. At the time of Barnard's visit, the distillery had two small, old pot stills, both holding about 1,000 gallons. Barnard was told that 'the distiller believes in using only small Stills to produce a rich thick whisky'. However, in the 1956 rebuild, these were replaced by three different stills, which were doubled up ten years later. Since 1956, Benrinnes has applied a form of triple distillation, which is not normally the way to make 'rich thick whisky'. Triple distillation usually achieves a lighter spirit of higher alcohol; Benrinnes new-make is around 76 per cent abv. Furthermore, the wash stills in particular, at 20,000 litres, could never be considered 'small stills'.

The three types of still at Benrinnes are the wash still, the low wines still and the spirit still. The first, 'strong heads' part of the wash still run goes straight to the spirit still, but everything else is distilled three times. Indeed, the weak feints at the end of the spirit still run are sent right back to the weak low wines receiver to have a further two distillations. This is a complicated system which is quite unique. Does it make a good whisky? Certainly the blenders seem to think so as Benrinnes is considered 'top class' and finds its way into the blends of Johnnie Walker, J&B and Dewar's. For a long time it was the main malt component of Crawford's Three and Five Star blends.

In recent years, a new single malt has appeared, called Stronachie. That was the name of a distillery in Perthshire, which closed in 1928. The provenance of Stronachie 12 year old single malt is a secret. Dewar Rattray, the producer, wanted a whisky that would closely match a 1904 sample from the original Stronachie distillery. They found a match somewhere, and rumour has it that it is Benrinnes. So Benrinnes may have an alter ego in the forensic reconstruction of whisky from a lost distillery.

Barnard reports that 'we adjourned to the office to refresh ourselves with a little of the Benrinnes Malt Extract to remove the dust from our throats.' That doesn't say very much, but then the dram can hardly have been very similar to what is produced these days (though even in 1855 the make was good enough to be ordered a year in advance). I was recently able to evaluate a 36 year old sample of Benrinnes, drawn from a bourbon hogshead. To the nose, it was a bountiful table, groaning under all kinds of exotic fruits, honey, fudge and crème brulée, and tastefully decorated with flowers and blossoms. A deeply satisfying melange of aromas with a taste to match; rich and sweet, a touch of mint, clove rock, marmalade and a long pepper finish. Sensually indulgent yet supplying dreams of heaven, this was another classic old Speyside fit for fallen angels.

THE ANGELS' SHARE (Extract)

Gordon Jarvie

From The Tale of the Crail Whale (Harpercroft 2006)

There's a zesty tang in the crystal air
With a haze of peat, pine and malt over Speyside
Ascending into heaven. Is this the angels' share
Rising on countless larks' wings, pride upon pride?

The mist over Speyside isn't any old mist
But smokes from Glenlivet, Knockando, Tamdhu,
Chivas Regal, Tomintoul, Glenallachie, Cardhu,
Glenfiddich, Macallan, Aberlour, to mention
   a few.

Caperdonich, Ben Riach, Tormore and
   Longmorn,
Balvenie, Glen Moray and Mortlach: on and on.
This is a world-class distillation,
A roll-call to tempt any angel's discrimination.

I survey all this and more
Sitting by the trig point of Ben Rinnes
Inhaling an almost celestial panorama,
The air thick with larks and angels.

CRAIGELLACHIE

CRAIGELLACHIE IS THE BEATING heart of Speyside, where the Fiddich runs into the Spey and roads radiate out to nearby centres of distilling — Aberlour, Keith, Dufftown and Rothes. Once Craigellachie was also an important railway junction and here the Spey runs gently under Telford's historic bridge, still elegant but no longer carrying traffic.

This small village has two art galleries and a trilogy of drinking establishments of great character and complimentarity — something for every shade of sophistication. The legendary Fiddichside Inn is a traditional, front parlour kind of pub, while the Craigellachie Hotel has the sumptuous Quaich Bar with over 700 malts, an Aladdin's cave for the serious whisky lover. Between these two in every sense is the Highlander, now in the competent hands of Duncan Elphick.

The distillery sits on the left as you take the road to Dufftown. If it is a warm day, the still room window shutters will be up and the big, fat, shiny stills are a pleasure to view — the most visible of all the Speyside stills. The distillery site is quite open and attractive as the various warehouses that used to hem it in were removed in 1991. Nonetheless, it is sad to see a distillery with no whisky maturing on-site. New-make spirit is sent to Cambus, as a result of the contract with the previous owners.

The company was first established in 1888, just a couple of years after Barnard toured the area. Charles Doig designed the distillery, which was completed in July 1891. The venture was a joint one between Alexander Edward and the larger than life Peter Mackie (a dynamic entrepreneur known as 'Restless Peter' among his staff). Peter Mackie later established White Horse Distillers Ltd, which company took over ownership of Craigellachie in 1916. Because of a long connection with the company, and having the name painted on the wall for many years, Craigellachie was referred to locally as 'the White Horse distillery' until quite recently.

The distillery was completely rebuilt in 1965, when the number of stills was doubled to the present four. In 1998, it was one of the four distilleries that went to Dewar's (Bacardi) as a result of the merging of Guinness and Grand Metropolitan. Dewar's have continued with a very positive investment and modernisation programme, and the milling operations and the mashing are completely computerised. The mash tun, installed in 2001, is a very modern, state-of-the-art Steineker full-lauter mash tun. The stainless steel top gleams like a spaceship and the underneath, with its radiating steel pipes, is futuristic and bewildering. This very impressive piece of equipment is housed in the old kiln room; the beautiful wooden roof above it is a curious and attractive contrast to the shining steel.

Not all the production equipment was washed away on this tide of modernisation. The eight washbacks, which were last changed in 1965, have all been recently replaced, but not with stainless steel. They are traditional wooden vessels in very attractive larch. Similarly, the distillery continues to use worm tubs for condensing the spirit, believing that any change here would affect the character of the whisky.

Distillery manager Jake Bremner came to work at Craigellachie in its centenary year, 1991. He told me that more than 90 per cent of the output (which is 2.7 million litres) goes into blends, such as White Horse and Dewar's. There are a few single malt expressions available from independent bottlers, and UDV produced a Flora and Fauna bottling at 14 years old which is increasingly hard to find. The current standard distillery expression is a 14 year old dram, which I found very palatable, with aromas of honey, shortbread and vanilla slices on a wooden baker's tray, tasting sweet and malty with a warming effect and a slight aftertaste of bitter orange.

LEAP GALLERY

A WEE DRAPPIE O'T (Extract)

Traditional

This life is a journey we a' hae to gang,
And care is the burden we carry alang —
Though heavy be our burden, and poverty
  our lot,
We'll be happy a' thegither owre a wee
  drappie o't.

Job, in his lamentation, said man was made to
  mourn,
That there was nae pleasure frae the cradle tae
  the urn;
But in his meditations he surely had forgot
The pleasure man enjoys owre a wee drappie o't.

When friendship and truth and good fellowship
  reign
And folk that are old can feel youthful again
When ilka heart is happy and worldly cares forgot
Is when we're a' met thegither owre a wee
  drappie o't.

GLENALLACHIE

YOU APPROACH GLENALLACHIE by heading west out of Aberlour and taking the Edinvillie road. The name means 'glen of the rocky place'. The distillery, completed in 1967, was the third to be designed by William Delmé-Evans, after Tullibardine (1947) and Isle of Jura (1963). Delmé-Evans acquired quite a reputation as a designer and architect of distilleries, some likening him to a latter-day Charles Cree Doig, though in terms of output he is a long way short. Certainly though, they were both involved in a period of renaissance in the world of whisky production. Delmé-Evans also ran a farm in Herefordshire. He famously had a runway constructed on Jura, bought a plane and learned to fly, so that he could commute efficiently between Herefordshire and Jura during the construction of the distillery on the island.

It is not recorded how he commuted to Speyside during the construction of Glenallachie, but the story is told that the construction workers welded his bicycle to a high beam as a practical joke after they became fed up with his fastidious attention to detail and his uncompromising standards. The workers' cottages adjoining the distillery had been half-constructed facing the wrong way and he insisted on having them dismantled and rebuilt. The buildings at Glenallachie are fairly obviously of 1960s architectural design, but they have at least been built in a traditional style, with whitewashed walls and grey slate roofs. The distillery has been described as 'motel-like', but I quite like it and wouldn't mind staying there a couple of nights.

Glenallachie was commissioned by Mackinlay McPherson Ltd (previously Charles Mackinlay & Co Ltd of Leith). Mackinlay had been part of Scottish and Newcastle Breweries since 1961 and they were looking for a fine, subtle, delicate, complex malt for blending purposes. Glenallachie, sadly, has never been bottled as a single malt, apart from a few versions made available by independent bottlers. From the outset it was a main component in Mackinlays, and later it became the backbone of the Clan Campbell blend. Scottish and Newcastle sold their whisky interests to Invergordon in 1985 and the distillery was then closed. Campbell Distillers took it over in 1989, when it was reopened and the capacity was increased, by doubling the number of stills from two to four. It is now part of the Pernod Ricard group.

The stills have bolted collars and, unusually, two 'man doors', one being considerably smaller than the other. The condensers are very unusual in being horizontal in position. The mash tun (10 tonnes of grist per mash) was apparently shipped over from Sweden and put together by Forsyths of Rothes. The mash tun and the stills look out through a picture window on a very pleasant view. The wash-backs are stainless steel, but among the most colourful I have seen, painted minty green with blood red and coffee coloured piping, and orange switcher engines on top. As one might expect, this is a highly automated distillery.

Production water comes from springs, while the cooling water comes from a pond, fed from a dam on the Lour Burn. This pond is an attractive feature in front of the distillery gates and ducks are often seen swimming there, perhaps because of the warm water from the condensers. At one time the distillery manager considered them his personal pets and sat vigil with a gun when foxes were around. It is also said that when the distillery was sold, these ducks were part of the inventory, all being individually valued; the joke was that the ducks cost all the money and the distillery came free of charge.

SIGH

THE AUTHOR'S EARNEST CRY AND PRAYER (Extract)

Robert Burns

Sages their solemn een may steek,
An' raise a philosophic reek,
An' phisically causes seek
In clime an' season;
But tell me whisky's name in Greek,
I'll tell the reason.

Scotland, my auld, respected mither!
Tho' whiles ye moistify your leather,
Till whaur ye sit on craps o' heather,
Ye tine your dam;
Freedom and whisky gang thegither
Tak' aff your dram!

THE MACALLAN

ALFRED BARNARD IS UNUSUALLY reticent about the Macallan distillery — only seven lines. Nothing is measured and there is a very ironic sentence: 'its internal arrangements are similar to the other Spey-side distilleries.' For what has become the Rolls Royce of malts from the whisky chateau, this is a bit disappointing. One suspects that Barnard did not enter past the distillery gates for some reason. I did get through the distillery gates. Indeed it turned out to be one of the most memorable distillery visits of my Speyside tour.

To stand on the lawn in front of Easter Elchies House is to enjoy the double thrill of history and geography. The view across the valley from the distillery is one of the most pleasing on the Spey. The Craigellachie Hotel peeks shyly from the trees away to the left and the ancient scurran-crested summit of Ben Rinnes towers over the mid-distance patchwork of fields and forests.

The house itself, now a shrine to the Fine and Rare series of vintage Macallans, is the setting for events and VIP and corporate entertaining. It was built in 1700 by Captain John Grant, though there would have been a house there for at least a century before that (there are records of it being plundered by a Covenanting army in the mid 17th century). The house was sold to the Seafield Estate in the 1750s and was renovated and extended (to 29 rooms) by Lord Seafield in 1857. By the 1960s it had once more fallen into disrepair, and it was restored to its original shape (removing the 1857 extensions) by the Board of Macallan between 1981 and 1985, at a cost of £500,000.

Next to Easter Elchies House is a very old holly tree, which may be as old as the house itself. In a recent programme of woodland regeneration, 1,000 oak saplings were planted on the estate. People were given a chance to buy a package of The Macallan Woodland Estate, which was a bottle of 12 year old along with one of the saplings. Each person who bought one will have a plaque bearing their name on their tree. I have heard that Macallan have applied for permission to construct a tree house in the grounds. This will be on a scale large enough for people to conduct tastings inside, and will be a unique distillery feature. They really do care about wood as their new 'story of oak' exhibition testifies.

The present visitor centre, converted in 2001 from gardeners' cottages, is the starting and finishing point for most visitors. Arriving at the distillery, the road runs between fields of barley; indeed, Macallan manage about 600 acres of their own barley here. They do not make a great thing about the terroir concept, but from 2003 they have casked spirit made from their own barley separately, to maintain its integrity. All Macallan is stored and matured on-site, in more than 20 warehouses, including one large new store which holds as much as all the others put together and is the biggest

single-roofed warehouse in Europe. It is in warehousing that most of the distillery workers are employed.

The barley used in making Macallan is mostly Golden Promise (approx 70 per cent; almost the entire stock of Golden Promise in Scotland). This is not a particularly high-yielding strain, but it gives the whisky its flavour. When you consider that the distillery has an annual output of around six million litres, this is clearly not a decision driven by accountants. Every step of the process is designed to achieve the desired characteristics of Macallan new-make spirit; sweet, oily and richly robust.

To achieve this output, the Macallan distillery works very hard. The mash tun converts seven tons of barley grist into 39 thousand litres of wort in three and a half hours, and it does this seven times a day, seven days a week. This, in turn, feeds into 16 stainless steel washbacks, which are atmosphere-vented, highly sterile, almost self-cleaning. During the 1980s, the company ran stainless steel and wooden washbacks together and said it could detect no appreciable difference. The distillery uses three types of fresh distillers yeast (complex fermentation leads to complex flavours), which have to be stored at below five degrees centigrade before being blended together to start the fermentation.

After 48 hours of fermentation, the wash finds its way to the still-house. Macallan has 21 stills, though only 15 are currently in use. With 15 stills operating, condensers inside the building and the sun shining through the large glass frontage, this can be a hot environment. The stillmen prefer it in the winter, when they can look out from their pleasantly warm environment and see crisp snow lying on Ben Rinnes. The larger wash stills are heated by gas, and each one supplies low wines at 21 per cent abv for the two spirit stills.

These are remarkable in their shape and size. They are the smallest stills in Speyside and are of simple, conventional design. There is nothing to encourage reflux and the spirit has an easy journey up the short necks and down the lyne arm. This makes for a fairly sinewy, robust spirit — coquettish elegance is not what Macallan are after. However, I was given some of the new-make to taste and was astonished at how sweet, fragrant and drinkable it was. Small stills probably allow more contact with copper in the way that small casks allow greater contact with wood. The stills are gas-fired and run slowly, and only about 15 per cent of the run is taken as the middle cut for filling into casks.

That 15 per cent is the raw product that meets the wood for its long sleep. Macallan's wood management policy is one of the most careful and considered in the whole of Scotland. Most of the casks employed at Macallan are butts and puncheons from Spain. The company has these made in Jerez, favouring European oak, *quercus robur*, rather than American, *quercus alba*. It loans them to Gonzalez

Byass for about three years, during which time they contain mostly Oloroso sherry. Then they are shipped back whole to Scotland and put to work in the distillery. Fino casks are used for the Elegenzia, and Macallan do fill (and have always filled) some American barrels and hogsheads.

In 2004, Macallan rebranded their whole range and unveiled the Fine Oak malts. This did not remove the traditional sherry-matured Macallan, but brought to the world an additional series of bourbon-matured expressions. At the moment, Macallan is the fourth best selling single malt in the world, having jumped from sixth place in recent years, and the rebranding is designed to move it up the ladder at least one more place. Sales of The Macallan have doubled in five years; this is a malt on the move.

At the end of my tour, I was entertained with a nosing and tasting of several from the range, accompanied by a PowerPoint presentation of the famous 'spider' tasting diagrams. This was a vertical tasting of great whiskies, soaring from the new-make through the 12 year old (pears and ginger), the 15 year old fine oak (toffee, rose and cinnamon), the flagship 18 year old (raisins, citrus and spice) and on into the heavens with the elegant, tingly 25 year old (dried fruit, citrus, sherbet mouth feel) and the 30 year old fine oak with its perfumed orange groves.

At that point, Bob Delgarno, Macallan's whisky maker, arrived on the scene and took me through to the adjoining room, where he and his assistant, Ian Morrison, concoct and alchemise, like wizards in some Harry Potter episode, the future expressions of The Macallan. Delgarno produced from the flowing sleeves of his star-covered robe an interesting 1975 vintage, then three further samples that may become single cask bottlings. Flying with the experts on an unsteady broomstick, I was rocketed into the stratosphere with samples of a 40 year old, a 50 year old and finally (sworn to secrecy) an even older expression.

Macallan have the most extensive portfolio of vintage expressions of the make of any distillery in Scotland. Few are privileged to do more than stare at these bottlings. I have been so privileged and will remember the occasion for a long time, my enjoyment not particularly diminished by the nagging regret that I didn't leave my car at home.

DAWN IN MACALLAN

Guy Heath

A cold wind is rising over the hill
A dream to surprise me and probably will
There's a wind on the heather there's a song on
*   the hill*
It's dawn in Macallan and everything's still.

Far down below so far I can't say
A river is winding in fine silver spray
Majestic and silent, it's both at one time
It's dawn in Macallan, the morning is mine.

Scotia, oh Scotia
I'll sing of your river and your glen
And I will tell a story
It's a tale of love and glory
And a song about Scotland and a friend.

Deep down below me deep down in the ground
There's never a murmur there's never a sound
And the water is rising so soft and so clear
It's day in Macallan the morning is here.

And the cold mist is lifting as it's warmed by
*   the sun*
The barley is yellow the morning's begun
A lady is singing as the stories unfold
It's day in Macallan the water is gold.

Scotia, oh Scotia…

But time is forever and time is a friend
My story's unwinding and never will end
My song has begun now a life of its own
It's night in Macallan the morning has flown.

And a cold mist is rising over the hill
A dream to surprise me and probably will
There's a wind on the heather, there's a song
*   on the mill*
It's night in Macallan and everything's still.

THE SPEYSIDE COOPERAGE

JUST OUT OF CRAIGELLACHIE on the road to Dufftown is the Speyside Cooperage. This family-owned business is the only surviving independent cooperage in Speyside. At one time there were three in Craigellachie alone. Some of the distilleries and whisky companies have their own coopers (when Barnard visited, they nearly all did) but there seems to be plenty of work for the cooperage at Craigellachie, in Speyside and beyond (they also provide casks for clients in England and abroad). The Speyside Cooperage has 10 coopers and three apprentices and handles millions of casks. The coopers seem to be on a piece-work contract and they handle these casks with amazing skill, ease and speed.

Mainly, they deal with American barrels (200 litres), hogsheads (250 litres) and butts (500 litres). I understand that the coopers are happy with all of these, but the traditional hoggies are the hardest to work (bourbon barrels remade into hogshead size are called dump hoggies). There are various other casks, including port pipes, puncheons and gordas; I was even shown a square cask that was commissioned by one of the companies but never actually used.

The Speyside Cooperage opened its visitor centre in 1992 and has an exhibition and information area, a viewing gallery, a shop and a delightful picnic area outside, where families can have lunch inside enormous barrel houses. From the viewing gallery, one can see the coopers in action as they deal with a seemingly endless flow of casks. The main job seems to be repairing casks, though they also create new ones. Repairing and rebuilding involve dismantling casks, removing spoiled staves or ends and replacing them. The staves are then planed, if necessary, and reunited, sometimes using reeds (harvested from the River Ouse) as a traditional form of gasket between the staves.

As well as the joinery and puzzle-building end of the task, casks are often charred on the inside to help the wood perform its function. The actual process can vary, from the light toasting preferred for European oak to the heavier charring that seems more suited to American oak. Incidentally, legend has it that the first man to discover the value of charring was Elijah Craig of Kentucky. Elijah was a businessman, an engineer, a Baptist preacher and a whisky maker. It is no surprise to learn that he came from Scottish stock. In fact, his family was reckoned to have emigrated from Craigellachie around 1750.

Exactly what happens to whisky in the wood is not entirely known but there is general agreement that up to two-thirds of the aroma, flavour and character of the whisky comes from the wood. The law states that unless it spends three years in oak it cannot be called whisky. Oak, as the ancient druids understood, is a wood with magical qualities. Charring or heating the wood has two effects: first, the carbon acts as a purifier, removing primarily that old miscreant, sulphur; second, molecular components of the oak contribute to the character of the whisky, in particular adding vanilla and coconut aromas and sweetness and dryness to the flavour.

Scotch whisky is very seldom filled into new wood as it impacts too heavily on the spirit. It is usually filled into second-hand casks that have previously held sherry or bourbon. Traditionally, sherry wood was most often used, but since the Second World War, bourbon barrels have been increasing in popularity. A used sherry cask can cost as much as £500, whereas a bourbon barrel is about £50, so only a handful of distilleries continue to favour sherry wood. In either case, a second-hand cask can add fantastic flavour value to the whisky matured within, though the more often a cask is used, the less the impact will be. A typical cask lifespan might be 50 to 60 years.

Oak is not actually an ingredient in whisky-making but it has a huge impact on the character of the final product. Craigellachie Cooperage is where tired and damaged casks are cared for, to be sent back into the system for further duty. Without the skill and expertise of coopers, our dram would be a pale thing, devoid of character and finesse, and, like gin, needing various flavourings to make it palatable. We owe them our gratitude.

PIPER MACNEIL (Extract)

Traditional

The whisky's guid, aye the whisky's grand,
A wee drappie o't'll dae ye nae harm,
An' Ah only wish that in my airms
Ah had a great big barrel o' Hielan whisky-o.

KNOCKANDO AND BALLINDALLOCH

The section of the Spey above Aberlour runs from the parish of Knockando to Ballindalloch Castle and the hill of Craggan More, below which the River Avon flows into the Spey from the upland areas. This beautiful part of Speyside has no substantial town but many attractive hamlets and an amazing string of distilleries.

**CARDHU
CRAGGANMORE
DAILUAINE
GLENFARCLAS
IMPERIAL
KNOCKANDO
TAMDHU
TORMORE**

Photo: Robin Laing

CARDHU

IN THE PARISH OF KNOCKANDO, about five miles upstream from Aberlour, there is a little corner of the Spey with a cluster of distilleries whose names sound like they should be written into a poem or a song — Tamdhu, Cardhu and Knockando. While the other two are right by the river, Cardhu stands in a more elevated position looking out across the valley of the Spey, with grand views of Ben Rinnes to the south.

Cardhu is the only one of Diageo's 16 distilleries in Speyside to have a visitor centre. A rather out-dated video on a small screen competes with the noise of the mill above and tells us poetically of how the mash tun rakes move 'like the flailing arms of some sea monster'. In fact, the mashing is done in a Lauter tun, the sea monster having been banished some time ago.

The water for distilling comes from springs in the Mannoch Hills and the malt is brought in by road. The two pagoda chimneys are still in evidence, the larger one now sitting on top of a corporate entertainment facility, where I'm sure hot air is hardly ever in evidence. The eight washbacks are of Scottish larch and fermentation here takes place over a leisurely 65 hours at an absolute minimum, and sometimes considerably longer, leading to a lighter character in the final spirit. Approaching the stills in Cardhu is like entering a temple — they are elevated and slightly aloof and the visitor has to look up with reverential gaze. The sweet,

fresh aromas wafting around the stillhouse lift the soul more immediately than incense in a Greek church at Easter.

Cardhu is jointly managed with the distilleries of Knockando and Cragganmore, and all three distilleries share the same staff. The visitor centre staff also provide a limited service to Cragganmore. I was lucky to be shown round Cardhu by Helen Gardiner. She has a refreshing enthusiasm for the product of Speyside in general and for the Cardhu dram in particular, which she describes as the quintessential Speyside malt. After nosing and tasting this sweet, fragrant and delicious whisky, it is hard to disagree with that.

Unfortunately, Cardhu has become a victim of its own success and demand for it has mushroomed to the point that the distillery cannot produce enough spirit. This has already led to Diageo's attempt to mix it with whisky from another distillery and describe it as Cardhu Pure Malt — a move that was successfully challenged by others in the industry. So what happens now is that Cardhu is only available in certain markets, notably France, Greece and especially Spain, where it is currently the number one best selling malt.

It is now unusual to see Cardhu on sale in the UK, though it is available at the distillery. It might be available in some specialist whisky shops but they will probably have bought it in from Spain and the price may well reflect that. Speyside, the home of Cardhu, goes without, while Spainside is awash with it and the lucky Spaniards can buy it for about one-third of the UK price. Then they generally drown it with ice and coca-cola. There is no justice in this world.

The origins of Cardhu are interesting. As is often the story in Speyside, illicit distilling preceded the licence. In this case it was carried out by John and Helen Cumming. John was a convicted smuggler who leased the farm at Cardow

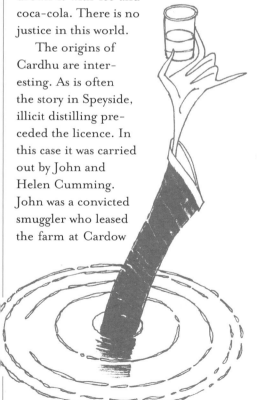

in 1811. We can be pretty sure he was plying his trade from there, for in 1824, following the Excise Act the previous year, he took out a licence. He died in 1846, when his son Lewis took over the business. When Lewis died in 1872 his wife, Elizabeth Cumming, took over in turn. She may well be the first woman on record to own and run a distillery.

Even then, the demand for Cardhu was greater than its supply. So what did Elizabeth do? Well, she didn't mix it with other stuff or ration it out to certain markets — she boldly decided to invest in the distillery by building a new one right next door, and in 1885 the new Cardhu went into production. Being a canny Scot, she sold the old distillery's equipment to William Grant, who was setting up Glenfiddich in Dufftown. Elizabeth was affectionately known as 'the Queen of the Whisky Trade'.

In 1893, she sold the distillery to Johnnie Walker and Cardhu became the central component of that blend, and may be part of the reason for the brand's phenomenal success. These days, it is likely that Cardhu is only a very small part of the malt contribution to Johnnie Walker. I have read that only 30 per cent of the two million litres of annual production is bottled as a single malt, but that seems unlikely. Incidentally, Johnnie Walker, the best selling blend in the world, was also withdrawn from the UK market for a few years in the late 1970s, and struggled to regain its position here when reintroduced.

Alfred Barnard visited Cardhu exactly at the time when the old distillery was about to be replaced by the new one, so his comments are of particular interest. Having walked all the way from the nearest station at Carron, he arrived with 'a mighty appetite, which was soon allayed by the well-known hospitality of Mrs Cummings.' It is interesting that she could look after guests so well in the midst of a change-over from one distillery to another. When I travelled to Cardhu, I decided to walk from Carron, too. I thoroughly enjoyed the walk and, like Barnard, arrived with a mighty appetite. As there was nothing at all available to eat or drink at the distillery (it is not that kind of a visitor centre) or anywhere nearby, I had to make do with an apple scrabbled out of the depths of my rucksack.

Barnard says that the experimental new-make had been judged by independent experts to be very similar to the character of the product of the old distillery, being 'of the thickest and richest description, and admirably adapted for blending purposes'. The quality of Cardhu today is not in doubt but it is likely that the character has changed considerably since 1887. Barnard talks of pot stills heated directly by furnaces and a peat-fired kiln — indeed peats from the Mannoch Hills were 'stored in a lofty shed, 100 feet long and 30 feet broad.' No wonder that

Barnard was told 'a single gallon of it is sufficient to cover 10 gallons of plain spirit and it commands a high price in the market.' The 'quintessential Speyside malt' means different things at different times.

I walked back to Carron with a dram of Cardhu inside me to lighten the load. It felt like it was still summer. Birds were singing and the sun dappled the Spey. Through the trees I saw a couple of two-person canoes drift by and heard calls and laughter as the river carried them downstream. I thought of the Lady of Shallot and of smoke and mirrors. I walked past the sad shell of Imperial distillery and thought of Camelot. The past can be as difficult to see into as the future and we are lucky to have people like Alfred Barnard, who give us windows to peer through.

All whisky lovers know that a malt can be enhanced or tainted by associations with and memories of previous experiences. Cardhu was the first whisky my wife and I drank together. For me, therefore, because of romantic associations, Cardhu will always be a lover's dram. Even when I try it alone, the nose is invigorating and evokes flowers and chocolates, spice, honey and perfumed shrubbery. It tastes delicious, goes down easy and one is never enough. And the delightfully contoured bottle will never slip through your fingers — a dram to hold on to all night.

HERE'S A BOTTLE

Robert Burns

Here's a bottle and an honest friend!
What wad ye wish for mair, man?
Wha kens, before his life may end,
What his share may be o care, man?

Then catch the moments as they fly,
And use them as ye ought, man!
Believe me, happiness is shy,
And comes not ay when sought, man!

CRAGGANMORE

THE ROAD TO CRAGGANMORE is much the same today as it was when Barnard took it westward from Carron to visit this delightful distillery, except that Barnard was lucky to be travelling in the days before the arrival of the motor car and its frightening roar. The scenery here, where the Avon flows into the Spey, will not have altered greatly and it is still the case that 'the beauty of the Spey is enhanced by the contrast it offers to the wild and rugged scenery around it.' Those words encapsulate what remains special about this entire area.

Cragganmore is Gaelic for 'the big rock' and is named after the hill that rises to 1,558 feet behind the distillery. In 1869, John Smith (the same John Smith who had previously leased Glenfarclas) applied for a lease from George Macpherson-Grant of Ballindalloch castle to build a distillery on his estate. Cragganmore was the first malt distillery to be built in Scotland in about 30 years.

It was also the first one to be sited next to a railway. The Strathspey Railway opened in 1863 and Cragganmore had its own siding close to Ballindalloch station. This proved very beneficial for moving casks from the distillery to the markets. John Smith was apparently a bit of a railway enthusiast, though being such a large man (21 stones) he always had to travel in the guard's van. Smith was still the proprietor when Barnard visited Cragganmore, though the entry ends with the words, 'It is with regret that we have to add, that since the above report was written, Mr John Smith has died.'

At the end of the century, the distillery was fortunate not to be affected by the Pattison's crash. Indeed, in 1902, it was given a confident rebuild under the designing hand of Charles Doig. The Smiths' reign came to an end in 1923 when the lease expired. The distillery then came under the joint ownership of the Macpherson-Grants of Ballindalloch and Peter Mackie of White Horse distillers. White Horse later became part of DCL.

Ballindalloch Castle is still owned by the Macpherson-Grants. These days it is open to the public, and it has a number of interesting features to reward the visitor, including gardens, a shop and tearoom, a golf course, a miniature railway, a collection of Wemyss China and an observation beehive. Barnard writes of passing 'the palatial entrance to the castle of Ballindalloch' and of its 'grand policies'. I am sure he would take the time to visit the castle if he were touring distilleries today.

There have been many changes at Cragganmore over the years (Barnard describes two water wheels) but the distillery still has a Victorian feel to it. It is probably quiet compared to the bustle that Barnard would have encountered, as the cooperage and the Excise offices have gone. The distillery today has considerably fewer workers than it then did, being currently operated by the same small team that looks after Knockando and Cardhu.

Other changes include doubling the number of stills from two to four in 1964 and converting from coal-firing to steam in 1972. The stills, incidentally, are unusual in having flattened tops. This feature goes back to the days of John Smith but is not clear whether they were designed that way because of the lack of head room in the still-house or as an unusual way of achieving reflux; whatever the reason, the shape has endured. One thing distillers are extremely reluctant to change is the shape and size of stills.

Barnard also tells us of a peat shed containing 'hundreds of tons of this valuable fuel'. Nowadays the phenolic content of Cragganmore is about 2ppm; in other words negligible, and the malting no longer takes place on-site. There is still some warehousing containing about 5,000 casks but, in common with many other distilleries in the group, most of the new spirit is taken away from the distillery at birth.

Cragganmore still has worm tubs and produces a new-make spirit that is relatively heavy and sulphurous in character. That character is lightened by maturation in mainly bourbon casks. The 12 year old Cragganmore is one of the six Classic Malts and as such has reached a far greater audience than it might have otherwise. In the second edition of the six, called the Distillers' Edition, Cragganmore is finished in port pipes and is more to my taste. It has plum jam, matchboxes,

COME IN NUMBER EIGHT...

orange and carnations on the nose and the taste is deliciously rich with spice, barley sugar and lots of toffee; smooth, luxurious and heady.

Cragganmore has also long been a fingerprint in the Grand Old Parr blend, which sells well in Asian markets. Old Parr apparently lived for 152 years and had eight wives. Once again we have evidence of the power of whisky to increase one's *élan vital*, a message not really necessary in Scotland as we all know about it already.

ON GUID SCOTS WHISKY (Extract)

George Bruce

E'en beggar bodies are fu' happy,
Whane'er o' ye they get a drappie,
In horn, or stoup, or timmer cappie,
    Tho' duds be scanty;
Yet blest as kings, they, owre the nappie,
    Forget ilk wantie.

But, what need further botheration,
I'm clear, a drap in moderation,
Has a' the wise's approbation;
    Then, guid Scots Whisky,
Mak' a' the bairns o' this auld nation
    'S leal hearts fu' frisky.

DAILUAINE

BARNARD'S ENTRY FOR 'Dail-Uaine' (he used the hyphenated form) is one of the longest for any Speyside distillery. He was clearly impressed, though it is difficult to say whether more by the distillery or its surrounding scenery. It is one of his most effusive and poetic appreciations of the landscape and natural surroundings of the Spey area. His superlative raptures are worth examination; the area around the Spey at Carron is surely just as beautiful today as it was in the 1880s, especially if you get a good day, as Barnard certainly did.

He describes for us:

one of the most beautiful reaches of the Spey... where we would fain have lingered for hours. Here the whole glory of the scenery below suddenly burst upon us, and new points of beauty presented themselves. Words can convey but a feeble idea of the enchanting loveliness of Strathspey as it now opened before us enclosed in its frame of hanging woods ... as we get our first glimpse of Dail-Uaine, nestling in one of the most beautiful little glens in Scotland. Never was there such a soft, bright landscape of luxuriant green... the whole scene is dainty enough for a fairy's palace... In this retired spot, far removed from noisy cities and prying eyes, surrounded by all that is beautiful and lovely in nature, is carried on the mystery of John Barleycorn, — his death, burial and resurrection. No wonder with these surroundings that the pure spirit emerging from such an Eden should be appreciated by mortals all the world over

That is only a part of Barnard's appreciatively lyrical description of the area around Dailuaine. It is such a shame that he was not equally poetic in his accounts of the whisky. At Dailuaine he was hassled by an impatient coachman, no doubt upset by having to wait longer than he was expecting, and you have the feeling that the farewell dram was a bit rushed, though greatly appreciated: 'On returning we find our coachman impatient and anxious, so, after quaffing a drop of the nectar, for which the distillery is famous, we trot merrily back in the cool of the evening to Craigellachie.'

It is particularly tempting to speculate about the dram he was given at Dailuaine. Once again he describes a distillery which only uses peat in the malting and kilning part of the process. He talks of: 'peat sheds, where we saw 2,000 yards of two-year-old peats, ready for immediate use.' Fascinatingly, in the same paragraph he describes the unusually lofty kiln roof: 'the roof, which is of the steepest pitch in Scotland rises to a height of 30 feet. This gives the Kiln its tower-like appearance. It is considered that height is of great advantage where peats are used solely, as it gives the malt its delicate aroma, without having to use coke to prevent the flavour being too pronounced.'

It would be wonderful to taste such a Speyside, surely entirely different from present-day Dailuaine. I cannot think of a distillery in the whole of Scotland which uses only peat for kilning, whatever the height of the roof!

That kiln roof is depicted in the two drawings which accompany Barnard's text on Dailuaine. Only three or four years later, it was replaced by an even more famous kiln roof, for Dailuaine was the very first distillery to be graced with the Chinese pagoda design of Charles Cree Doig, which he called the Doig Ventilator. Presumably, with the stronger draw of Doig's design, it was not necessary to have such a lofty kiln roof. From this point onwards, pagodas became the standard design and their familiar shape littered the landscape of Scotland. They are still seen in many places where malting is no longer carried out, are often used as a design motif in modern distillery projects and are retained as brand images by a number of companies. Most unfortunately, a serious fire in 1917 destroyed the original Dailuaine pagoda kiln, which otherwise would surely now be as big an attraction as the Forth Bridge.

It is ironic that so much of the distillery was destroyed by fire because the fire fighting equipment was one of the things that most impressed Barnard and he writes at length about the 'very complete arrangements for extinguishing fire'. Obviously they were not complete enough! In fact the distillery suffered a further significant fire in 1959.

JOHN BARLEYCORN

Dailuaine had the first of its major rebuilds just before Barnard's visit: 'Within the last few years nearly the whole of the distillery has been rebuilt on a larger and more modern style, and the work now contains all the latest improvements in the art of distilling.' He was particularly impressed with the 'new patent screening machines' and was surprised to learn that 'even home-grown barley sometimes contains foreign objects.' The distillery had 'four of the largest Grist Hoppers we have seen in the North of Scotland' and 'a Steel's Mashing Machine... composed of solid brass.' In 1886, Dailuaine had spirit stills with a capacity of 700 gallons (about 3,200 litres). Barnard says 'Messrs Mackenzie prefer small Stills to large ones, being convinced from long experience that they make better whisky.' The spirit stills today are 10 times the size, at 32,000 litres; small stills might make better whisky, but large ones make more.

Dailuaine is a very active, functional distillery these days. It produces 2.5 million litres of whisky per annum, most of which goes into Johnnie Walker blends. It has a dark grains plant, which, dating from 1965, is one of the earliest to have been installed at a malt distillery. Dailuaine also has a common effluent treatment works, or 'bio plant' which processes the spent lees and pot ale from ten distilleries. Dailuaine deals with 3,000 tonnes of pot ale and 920 tonnes of draff every week. It is a busy place. Yet there is something of a backwater air

about it. Part of that is because of the physical environment; away from the main road in a rather closed in, wooded valley, far from the hurly burly and the madding crowd. That was part of the charm that appealed to Barnard. At Carron, nearby, is the sleeping giant of Imperial, which was once part of the same enterprise, Dailuaine-Talisker Distilleries Ltd. The phoenix and the sleeping giant, side by side.

Close by the distillery ran the arterial route of the Strathspey Railway. A siding linked Dailuaine and Imperial distilleries to the main line. Dailuaine was another of the Speyside distilleries with its own pug locomotive. The engine shed is still there but the puggie, Dailuaine No 1, made by Barclay of Kilmarnock (home of Johnnie Walker), ran for the last time in 1970. It was sent to the Strathspey Railway Association at Boat of Garten and is now on display at Aberfeldy distillery, home of the House of Dewar visitor centre. Back at Dailuaine Halt, nowadays only occasional ramblers and walkers quietly stroll over the Spey, where steam engines once thundered by.

Within the confines of Dailuaine, one sees rows of Victorian dunnage warehouses, strong, granite-built buildings with crow-stepped gables, now apparently lying empty and disused. In another part of the plant, the old maltings also lie abandoned. Between 1959 and 1983, Dailuaine had Saladin box maltings. The old malting floors stretch like a football pitch of empty, unused space under an impressive vaulted ceiling of the most intricate wooden beams; a remnant of an age of traditional skills and craftsmanship. Somehow these relics of earlier days evoke a sense of loss, even if only in the less rational part of a poet's brain.

In the very early days, Dailuaine was the site of illicit stills, particularly those operated by James Grant. Barnard's account of the tales of smugglers' ghosts is very amusing:

> A popular legend has it that the midnight wanderer may yet see evidences of their craft, and that the darker the night and the wilder the weather the more likely is he to stumble across the haunted bothy, which is situated in a rocky cavern in a ravine through which rushes one of the Dail-Uaine Burns. There the Still-fires are seen weirdly sparkling like eyes of diamonds, and the ghosts of the departed smugglers busy at their ancient avocations.

Dailuaine was officially founded in 1851 by William Mackenzie, a local farmer. He died in 1865 and for the next 14 years the distillery was run by his widow, with the help of one James Fleming. In 1879, the widow's son, Thomas Mackenzie, became old enough to take over control and James Fleming built his own distillery in Aberlour. Dailuaine was rebuilt around 1885 and became one of the largest of the distilleries in the area. In 1898 it joined with Talisker to become Dailuaine-Talisker Distilleries Ltd. When Thomas Mackenzie died in 1915, the business was bought by a consortium including Buchanan, Dewar's and Johnnie Walker. Dailuaine became a subsidiary of DCL and is now one of Diageo's many distilleries.

The most unusual things I saw there were the two stainless steel condensers (the other four being copper). I have no idea what the tubes inside are made of, but I did wonder about the impact on the whisky, as I believe Tormore tried stainless steel in their distilling equipment and were forced to revert to copper. The whisky is available in three expressions from the company: the Flora and Fauna with a badger on the label, the Cask Strength Limited Edition and as one of the Rare Malts series. Otherwise it can sometimes be found under the logos of independent bottlers. I recently wrote a tasting note for a Scotch Malt Whisky Society bottling of Dailuaine which summed it up as 'A beautiful, warm, smile-inducing dram to curl up with on frosty nights, with thick woolly socks and a log fire.'

THE AUTHOR'S EARNEST CRY AND PRAYER (Extract)

Robert Burns

Paint Scotland greetin owre her thrissle;
Her mutchkin stoup as toom's a whissle:
An' damn'd Excisemen in a bustle,
Seizin' a stell,
Triumphant, crushin't like a mussel
Or limpet shell!

GLENFARCLAS

THE SPIRIT OF INDEPENDENCE

GLENFARCLAS DISTILLERY LIES NEAR the village of Marypark, about four miles west of Aberlour on the A95. The River Spey, which is hidden from view, is about two miles away. What is definitely not hidden from view is the towering hulk of Ben Rinnes — as you leave the main road and head up the drive to the distillery, the ben fills the view. Glenfarclas means 'valley of the green grass'; nearby is Tomfarclas, 'hill of the green grass'. It all sounds rather green, but Ben Rinnes provides a slide show of changing colour — green in the spring, purple in the summer, red in the autumn and occasionally white in the winter, while at any time of year it can turn blue in the haze, grey in the mist or black in a cauldron of hairy storm clouds.

About a year before my visit to Glenfarclas, I had the pleasure of having lunch with John Grant (chairman), Ian McWilliam (marketing executive) and their Swiss importer Rolf Lang, in Luzern. When I visited the distillery, John was away on business but Ian kindly showed me around. The history of Glenfarclas is very much the story of six generations of the Grant family. John Grant, born on Speyside 200 years ago, and his son George established the family business. Each generation of this distilling family since has been either a George or a John. These Grants are not related to either of the other Speyside distilling Grant families.

But to begin at the very beginning, Glenfarclas distillery was established on Recherlich farm in 1836 by Robert Hay. When Hay died in 1865, John Grant, who had developed a prize-winning herd of Aberdeen Angus cattle, took on the farm. The agreement included the purchase of the farm distillery, at a price of £519 19s. For the first four years, the distillery was leased to John Smith, but when he left in 1869 to build Cragganmore, the Grants decided to take over the distilling themselves.

The rest is history. However, distilling is seldom free from the vagaries of markets and economic cycles, and Glenfarclas distillery was adversely affected, perhaps more than most, by the whisky crash of 1898, as Pattison & Co of Leith had a half share in the Glenfarclas-Glenlivet Distillery Co. The distillery had just been rebuilt the previous year, doubling output, and the family was not going to give up that easily. Brothers John and George had to sell their entire stock of whisky and start again to see the company through that difficult period. Hard work and vision saw the company slowly prosper in the early decades of the new century.

As you might expect with a distillery that lies very much in the shadow of a mountain, that mountain provides the water source, both from natural springs and the Green Burn. In the last year or two, the water supply has been very tight and production has actually had to stop once. Scotland's whisky industry benefits from her particular climate conditions and especially from plentiful rainfall. Perhaps as global warming becomes more of an issue, such water supply problems will be faced more often.

Some of the Glenfarclas equipment is unusual. Instead of the usual Porteus or Boby mills, here you find a large mill of an entirely different dimension. This is a five-roller Bühler Mill, made in Uzwil, Switzerland and described as 'the Rolls Royce of mills'. This work horse can mill eight tonnes of malt an hour and has now completed 30 years of service at Glenfarclas without a problem.

The mash tun takes 16.5 tonnes of grist, and at 10 metres diameter, is one of the biggest anywhere in the industry. The 12 washbacks are of stainless steel, though the lids are wooden. Each one has a capacity of 45,000 litres, usually filled to 41,500 litres. The six stills are also substantial in size, the wash stills having a capacity of 23,000 litres. These stills are relatively rare in being gas-fired.

The company experimented with steam heating in 1980 but found that it adversely affected the character and body of the spirit and so reverted to direct-firing. Direct-firing needs rummager chains to stop any burnt deposit sticking to the bottom and this means that stills usually have a shorter lifespan. The price of copper makes this a significant issue however, but sometimes the sacrifice required for progress and economic benefit is too great. This says a lot about the philosophy of Glenfarclas and must raise a question as to whether the character of the whisky has been altered at any of the many distilleries that did change to steam. Steam heating is reckoned to lead to greater consistency of production, but it may be that the enormous size of the Glenfarclas stills helps to achieve a consistency that smaller direct-fired stills might not manage.

Glenfarclas has an interesting wood policy. Approximately two-thirds of Glenfarclas is filled into (mainly Oloroso) sherry casks supplied by a family firm based north of Seville. The other third goes into 'plain oak', which basically means second fill bourbon. Glenfarclas eschews first fill casks for their single malt expressions as they make the whisky too sweet and oily. This ratio of sherry to bourbon is reflected in most of the Glenfarclas bottlings. The big Oloroso influence means that Glenfarclas can say with complete honesty that they never have to use caramel for colouring. Every one of the approximately 55,000 casks in their 30 traditional dunnage warehouses is tracked by computer records. It is a great privilege to stand in these warehouses and see so many fat, beautiful casks with pedigrees down the years since about 1952.

The distillery stopped malting in 1972 and the pagoda now graces the entrance to the visitor centre. One of the interesting features of this visitor centre is the board room, which is lined with wooden panels salvaged from the ocean-going liner SS *Empress of Australia* (which, incidentally, started out life as the SS *Tirpitz*). It was in this sumptuously panelled room that Ian McWilliam and I concluded my visit with a tasting of some of the company's fine products.

Ian poured me a glass of new-make spirit to demonstrate its pear and cherry blossom character. Then he offered me a 9 year old sample from a plain oak cask and a 10 year old sample from a first fill sherry cask by way of demonstrating the contrasts. Samples like these occasionally appear in single cask bottlings but generally they are married together for the various expressions of Glenfarclas. The most common of these are the 10, 12, 15, 21, 25 and 30 year olds, some of which we also sampled. There is also a 40 year old, which is becoming a legend in whisky nosing circles because of Michael Jackson's description of the colour as 'deep amber, with a yellow suggestion of a gibbous moon'.

Some of the vintage Glenfarclas expressions are undoubtedly special, particularly for those who appreciate the sherry influence upon old whiskies (chocolate, fruit cake, oranges, prunes, spice, nuts etc), but for a very reasonably priced whisky of depth and character, it would be hard to beat the Glenfarclas 105 (105 proof = 60 per cent abv). First released in 1968, this was a pioneering step into the presentation of cask strength whisky. It was also a cask of Glenfarclas, back in the early 1980s, that started off

SPEYSIDE ▷

the Scotch Malt Whisky Society. Now-adays, company policy means that there are very few independent bottlings of Glenfarclas and those that do exist do not display the distillery name. I have seen a 10 year old 'Glen Montana' in the Art Deco Hotel Montana in Luzern, Switzerland, that had Glenfarclas on the label in smaller print, but that was an arrangement between the hotel and Glenfarclas to celebrate the 10th year of the hotel's Louis Bar.

Glenfarclas 105, with its crashing waves of sherry aromas and its memorably masculine taste explosion is one of the best value drams on the market. It can be an after dinner denouement or a reviving hit when out in the cold. I shared some with a friend on a bench by the side of the Spey and it seemed that the tumbling, rushing river was a song of joy scouring its way into my heart forever.

This is now one of the very few Scottish distilleries still in family owner-ship. There is no reason to suppose that a distillery run by a family will always fare better than one run by a multinational corporation, but it is good to see 'the Spirit of Independence' doing its own thing and putting quality and tradition above profit and economic streamlining.

At the time of my visit, John Grant was in Paris unveiling a new 50 year old Glenfarclas, which is sold along with an invitation to the distillery to sample the dram in case the owner does not want to open his or her bottle. I believe they are about to release a series of vintage bot-

tlings covering every year from 1952 to 1998. Not many distilleries could do that and it may be an industry first. It makes you feel that there is something solid and dependable at Glenfarclas.

Barnard's entry for Glenfarclas is rel-atively short; it is quite possible that they arrived in the late afternoon from Cardhu and were running short of time. He says that 'without the tall chimney stack we should have taken it for a scat-tered farm-holding', which a few years before, it had been. He describes a barley barn, malt barn, kiln and cooperage, all of which are now gone. At that time, seven warehouses held 2,000 casks, whereas now there are 30 warehouses with about 55,000 casks. Annual output, which was 50,000 gallons, is now poten-tially 3,000,000 litres, though actual output is currently considerably less.

These things have changed, but his poetic description of the scenery could apply today. He describes the place, away from the pleasant pastoral of the river, as 'not beautiful' and 'unlovely', but 'strange, gigantic and sublime'. As they travelled towards Glenfarclas, 'it was a most peculiar day, a languid sunshine pervaded the hazy atmosphere, creating a vagueness in the landscape. The mist stole in and out the crags and buttresses of Benrinnes', creating a 'weird sight' in this 'lonely waste'. These words sound like Tennyson's description of Ulysses and his companions arriving at the land of the Lotus Eaters. The uplands of Speyside often have that slightly spooky, magical quality, but it is not the fruit of the Lotus that tempts us to leave behind the burdens and responsibilities of life, but the juice of the Barley.

GLENFARCLAS (Extract)

Anon (thanks to Ian McWilliam)

If on life's seas of trouble
You're tossed boatless and barkless,
Your courage will double
From a drop of Glenfarclas.

If you're houseless and landless,
And poundless and parkless,
You'll care not twa candles
If you've got some Glenfarclas.

If you're ragged and bootless,
And hatless and sarkless,
You'll feel it nae doot less
If you've plenty Glenfarclas.

If you're bankrupt and beggared,
And hopeless and warkless,
Your lot will be sugared
By a waught o Glenfarclas.

IMPERIAL

IMPERIAL DISTILLERY WAS YET another of the 21 distilleries built in Speyside during the 1890s whisky boom. It lies in the beautiful setting of Carron, surrounded by forest-clad hills, on the north bank of the Spey, between Knockando and Dailuaine distilleries. The railway was a significant factor in choosing the site but that railway was dismantled and now forms the peaceful setting of the Speyside Way.

Construction began in 1897, the year of Queen Victoria's Diamond Jubilee, hence the name 'Imperial'. Charles Doig designed Imperial and gave it an impressive gilt crown on one of its pagodas. Both crown and pagodas have now disappeared. Unusually, Doig chose to have Imperial built using Aberdeen red brick, which looks as fresh today as it would have done a hundred years ago.

Inauspiciously, one worker was killed in November 1897 when scaffolding collapsed. Production commenced in 1898, the year of the Pattison's scandal, and Imperial closed in 1899 after only a few months' activity. Twenty years of silence followed, until distilling recommenced in 1919 for six years. After 30 more years of silence (though the massive maltings continued to operate), the distillery was reopened in 1955 with new equipment (and no crown), and then extended from two stills to four in 1965. It closed again in 1985 but reopened four years later, and stayed in operation until Allied Distillers mothballed it in 1998. Imperial has thus spent more than half of its life sleeping.

Imperial was built by Dailuaine-Talisker Distilleries Ltd in order to keep up with demand but by 1916 the company had been running at a loss for some years and was acquired by a consortium, which became DCL in 1925. In 1955, ownership transferred to Scottish Malt Distillers, and to Allied Distillers in 1989. Pernod Ricard acquired Allied in 2005.

Imperial single malt is rare and Michael Jackson describes it as underrated. Most bottlings have come from independents, though a few years ago Allied bottled a cask strength 15 year old from bourbon barrels. Rather surprisingly, for most of Allied's years of ownership Imperial was assigned to Black Bottle, which was supposed to contain mainly Islay malts.

From the beginning, water from the Ballintomb Burn was used for production, cooling and driving the water turbine. The distillery dam provided recreation in the 1930s for summer galas of the Caledonian Swimming Club of Aberdeen, and for soldiers during the Second World War, when the distillery was requisitioned by the army to provide accommodation for troops and act as a military store. Apparently some soldiers were quite keen on throwing hand grenades into the dam; hopefully not at the same time as the swimming club members were in the water.

Dealing with effluent has always been a problem and is probably the reason Imperial closed in 1925. In 1955, the first full-scale effluent treatment plant was built there, though more recently, Allied preferred to tanker pot ale away. Hot water from the condensers was channelled round a series of walls to allow it to cool sufficiently to enter the Spey. If the distillery were to reopen now, water supply and disposal of waste would be among the main challenges, though it is unlikely that these would be insurmountable.

Today, the massive stills (some of the biggest anywhere) sit in a row like Buddhas in a ruined temple. Every spring, a migration of toads comes through the still-house, in at the back and out through the front door. They seem incapable of going round the building and if the door is not open they get stuck. Even now, the owners make the necessary arrangements for them. The annual march of toads seems to be something the distillery can cope with, but the relentless march of time might prove more of a challenge.

To see it silent in such a beautiful setting is sad and one can't help thinking of the Sleeping Beauty. Imperial only ceased operating in 1998 but it is frightening to see what nature can do to a site after a few years. This is really crunch time for Imperial distillery. It was on the point of being sold by Allied in 2005 but new owners Pernod Ricard stopped the sale. No decision has yet been made about its future. With a bit of work it could still be put back into production, but another couple of years might see it pass beyond the point of no return.

PEGGY ON THE BANKS O' SPEY

Traditional

Peggy on the banks o' Spey
She's aye sae blithe an' cheery O.
She looks sae shy as I pass by
She fain wad be my dearie O.

On yonder knowes the heather grows
The birdie's a' sing bonnie O.
They sing sae sweet that I lang tae meet
My Peggy in the morning O.

Bleaching greens mak lasses clean
Their claes they a' shine bonny O.
They shine sae sweet that I lang tae meet
My Peggy in the gloaming O.

Some nicht I'll try as I pass by
And wed her frae her daddy O.
I'll kiss her ower and ower again
And row her in my plaidie O.

KNOCKANDO

IN 1898, JOHN TYTLER THOMPSON, a self-made whisky broker from Elgin, got Charles Doig to design him a distillery at Knockando. The distillery was built of locally quarried granite, which has a pink quality. Nowadays, that quality is enhanced spectacularly by the harling, which is painted in the most striking salmon pink. With its bright flags flying under a blue sky, it was quite a sight when I visited. The setting, right on the banks of the Spey, is amazing.

In a now-familiar tale, the hopeful start was immediately crushed by the Pattison's scandal and Thompson was unable to sell any of his whisky. Within a couple of years, he had been forced to sell the distillery to W & A Gilbey's, who acquired it for £3,500. Thompson seems to have been one of those guys who has great ideas but bad timing. After losing Knockando, he took his family to Australia, where he made a spectacular failure of a succession of enterprises, including farming, vintnering and gold mining. These were all things that would later bring riches to others but not to him.

So it was with whisky-making at Knockando; Gilbey's invested in the distillery and put it back into production in 1904. They already owned Glen Spey and Strathmill and their primary blend was Spey Royal. In 1905, Knockando was linked by a siding to the railway and soon after became the first distillery in Speyside to have electricity. In 1962, Gilbey's merged with United Wine Traders to become IDV, eventually becoming part of the Justerini & Brooks stable, and since then Knockando has been a component of J&B Rare. Justerini & Brooks later became part of Grand Metropolitan Hotels Ltd, now owned by Diageo. The distillery doubled its capacity in 1969, just after the maltings were removed, and soon after that the Knockando single malt was released. By the early 1990s it had become one of the top ten best sellers in the world.

The present manager is Innes Shaw, whose great grandfather was a joiner who helped in the construction of the distillery. I first met Innes in 1996 when I was walking the Speyside Way and just happened to pop my head round the door. He sent me and my companion on our foot-weary way with some leaflets and a couple of miniatures each — that day Knockando was a great reviver! I met Innes again more recently and was given a tour of the distillery and a dram in the visitor centre.

An old warehouse has been converted into quite a substantial visitor and event facility. Interesting photographs line one of the walls. I asked Innes about the ones that showed him, in his kilt, meeting Margaret Thatcher. Apparently, in 1985, Justerini & Brooks received the Queen's Award for Export Achievement, and that explained the visit from the Iron Lady. There was a serious security sweep and two policemen stayed in the distillery overnight. Thatcher was given the billionth bottle of J&B Rare and a personal tour of the distillery by Innes Shaw. It is rumoured that Knockando has a wardrobe of 40 kilts so that visiting groups from overseas can have a go at dressing up like Scotsmen, but Innes assured me that the kilt he was wearing in the photograph was his own. Thatcher was not the first Prime Minister to go to Knockando; Ramsay MacDonald, who came from Lossiemouth, opened a flower show there in the 1930s.

Knockando has attractive pine and larch washbacks and a warm, dark patina on the large stills (lamp-glass wash and boil-ball spirit in shape) but the really interesting things are the beauty of the setting outside and one or two of the items in the nearest warehouse. For example, there is a cask, racked on its side, with glass ends. Through the glass, enhanced by a light behind it, one can see what is normally never seen — whisky maturing in the wood. Behind an impressive iron gate is a vault of 128 casks which were vatted together in 1994 to cel-

ebrate the 500th anniversary of the first recorded reference to whisky-making in Scotland, made by Friar John Cor. One cask from every distillery in Scotland went into the mix and, as 12 of them were grain whisky, the result was a rather special blend, called J&B Ultima. The casks on

display are a colourful and fascinating collection.

The distillery records show that around a hundred years ago, most Knockando was filled into sherry butts, with some ending up in Madeira and Marsala casks and port pipes. Now about 90 per cent is filled into bourbon barrels. This reflects both changes in the second-hand cask market and the requirements of J&B Rare, but it would be fascinating to compare the tastes of then and now. That was never going to be possible, though I was given a couple of samples by Innes, back in the reception centre. Knockando is always bottled as a vintage, showing the dates of distillation and bottling. This is supposed to mean that casks are only married together for bottling when they are 'ready', whatever the actual age might be. Between 12 and 15 years old is the standard. Knockando is not readily available from independent bottlers.

Daylight was fading as I sat there, in the easy company of Innes Shaw, looking out over the wooded banks of the Spey, cradling a dram of fine whisky in my hand. I was reluctant to depart, but I had something else to do, as no doubt Innes also had, though he was very hospitable. I left the building as dusk shrouded the river valley, robbing the colour from the flags and the pink walls, leaving the 'small black hillock' of Knockando silhouetted against a livid, bruise-coloured sky.

JOCK STEWART

Traditional

Oh my name is Jock Stewart
I'm a canny gaun man
but a rovin' young fellow I've been

So be easy and free,
When you're drinking with me,
I'm a man you don't meet every day.

I have acres of land
I have men at command
but I've always a shilling to spare

So be easy and free...

I took out my gun
and my dog for a shoot
along the banks of the Spey

So be easy and free...

So come fill up your glass
of whisky or beer
and whatever the cost I will pay

So be easy and free...

TAMDHU

FROM MARYPARK, the road crosses the Spey at Blacksboat and winds its way round towards Tamdhu distillery. At various points here one can enjoy the finest vistas of the strangely named Hill of Phones on the south bank, and beyond that the bald and imposing Ben Rinnes. Approaching from the opposite direction, one passes through the sleepy villages of Archiestown and Knockando.

The Tamdhu-Glenlivet distillery was built in 1897 to a design by Charles Doig. It was founded by a group of business-men, including William Grant, agent of the Caledonian Bank in Elgin, and Robertson & Baxter, the Glasgow firm of blenders. The following year it was incorporated into Highland Distilleries Co Ltd, which still owns the distillery.

The site, by the Spey, was chosen for its proximity to the railway and for the water supply from the Knockando Burn. Almost immediately there arose disputes about the water supply and the company now uses water from the Tamdhu Spring, which rises under the distillery itself. The doors closed on Tamdhu in 1927 for 20 years. It was reopened after the war with a new effluent treatment plant and slowly began to rebuild its reputation. This obviously went according to plan because the production increased steadily, with the number of stills doubling to four in 1972. Three years later the distillery was practically rebuilt and the stills increased to six.

Tamdhu's malting facility is of con-siderable interest. It is probably the biggest in any malt whisky distillery and contains perhaps the only surviving example of Saladin maltings, designed by a Frenchman in the late 19th century. These were installed at Tamdhu in 1958. Saladin boxes were also in use at Balmenach, Imperial and Glen Ord, but Tamdhu's are the only ones remaining.

Thanks to this malting facility, Tamdhu not only meets all its own malt needs but also supplies malted barley to other distilleries in the group, especially Glenrothes and Macallan. The barley used by Tamdhu and Glenrothes is mainly Optic, while Macallan continues to favour Golden Promise. Whichever strain is used, it all comes from Scotland, usually from Angus or the Black Isle, as well as from local farmers. 16,000 tonnes of barley goes through Tamdhu maltings every year and every load has to be checked for size and viability as well as for grain weevils and saw-toothed grain weevils, whose ugly photographs grace the walls like wanted posters so that the workers might recognise them if they appear. If even one of these miscreant intruders was to be found in a load of malted barley, that entire load would be rejected.

The barley is steeped in the usual way (in cast iron steeps, soon to be replaced with stainless steel), but then instead of being spread out on a malting floor it is hosed as slurry into long Saladin boxes. Tamdhu has 10 of these and two are filled every day. Within each box is a sliding gantry, from which is suspended a series of metal turners, like giant corkscrews, that turn as the gantry slowly rakes them through the four feet deep bed of germinating barley. Each box is about 60 feet long and the gantry takes 10 hours to get from one end to the other. During this time, warm moist air is passed up through the perforated mesh in the Saladin box floor. It takes about four days for the germination to reach the required stage.

Once germination is complete, the malted barley is hoovered out of the box and sent to the kiln. This part of the process still involves a bit of manual shovelling, to guide the malt into the suction pipe. It looks like hard work, though probably not hard enough to give anyone the con-

dition of 'monkey shoulder', which maltmen suffered from in the old days.

Sandy Coutts, the distillery manager, allowed me a look into the Seager kiln. This kiln fills and empties itself and blows hot air through the barley to dry it. The air is pre-heated by waste hot water from the condensers and kilning time is about half that of a conventional kiln. As the door opened, the updraught poured thorough the opening, so that it was like standing before a turbocharged hairdryer. A tiny fire, smoored with damp peat dross, trickles smoke up into the kiln. This is to provide an almost token phenolic content of 1ppm.

Tamdhu has a Porteus malt mill, like many other distilleries, but this one is slightly unusual in having fluted rollers. It has nine huge Oregon pine washbacks — perhaps the biggest I have ever seen, each holding 65,000 litres. The stills are straightforward in design, with no obvious reflux mechanism, though they are quite large at 22,000 litres (wash) and 18,600 litres (spirit) capacity. There are 12 dunnage and one rack warehouses on-site, housing the equivalent of 25,000 butts.

The Tamdhu distillery produces 2.2 million litres of spirit a year (though its capacity is twice that). The new-make is very fruity in character. A large proportion of the matured malt finds its way into the Famous Grouse blend and the Famous Grouse Vintage Malt, as well as a few other blends. The standard Tamdhu single malt is bottled with no age statement and is particularly popular in the French market. I understand that 18 year old and 25 year old versions are soon to be released. Tamdhu can also often be found in independent bottlings. The Scotch Malt Whisky Society, for example, has bottled at least 40 casks of Tamdhu, which have proved highly popular, with their typical balance of syrupy, toffee sweetness, fruit and spice.

JOHN BARLEYCORN (Extract)

Robert Burns

John Barleycorn was a hero bold
Of noble enterprise.
For if ye do but taste his blood,
'Twill make your courage rise.
'Twill make a man forget his woe;
'Twill heighten all his joy;
'Twill make the widow's heart to sing,
Though the tear were in her eye.

Then let us toast John Barleycorn,
Each man a glass in his hand,
And may his great prosperity
Never fail in old Scotland.

TORMORE

THE PEARL OF SPEYSIDE

There is something precious about Tormore. Somewhere in the hills above, its water comes from the fabled Loch an Oir ('Loch of Gold'), while just below, where the Achvochkie Burn meets the Spey, used to be a favoured spot for fishing pearls from the fresh-water mussels. The middle reaches of the Spey still contain millions of these molluscs and this is considered one of the most important breeding sites in the whole of the UK. Fishing for these pearls, which adorn both the Scottish and the British crown jewels, is now illegal. Tormore distillery has the capacity to pump cooling water up from the Spey if it ever needs it — though this has not been done for more than 15 years — so the claimed connection between the distillery and the Spey pearl is not unreasonable.

Tormore is a relatively modern distillery, built between 1958 and 1960. It is often described as the first malt distillery to be built in Scotland in the 20th century, but in fact it was preceded by Tullibardine (1949) and Glen Keith (1957). There is no doubt, however, that the opening of Tormore was seen at the time as a significant event. It had been commissioned by an American company, Schenley Industries Inc, which owned Long John Whisky. It is said that no expense was spared in the construction of Tormore, and it was intended to be a showcase distillery from the start.

The well respected architect Sir Albert Richardson was chosen to design Tormore. He had been a president of the Royal Academy and had designed various buildings, including the Manchester Opera House. He was an expert on Georgian architecture and had a style that was a synthesis of the traditional and the modern. Tormore fits with that approach and now has listed building status.

The building has a lofty spaciousness about it. At the time of its opening, it had some fun poked at it for being too churchlike, because of its tall arched windows. Inside, it reminds me of that other whisky cathedral, Glenrothes. So spacious was the design that, only 12 years after its construction, it was able to double in capacity from four stills to eight without having to expand the building. The distillery had a number of unusual aspects, including the use of Kemnay granite and a very expensive copper roof. The chimney was to have been built in the shape of a whisky bottle, but that particular extravagance was abandoned.

The building next to the main distillery is graced with a clock tower which plays four traditional Scottish tunes every hour, including 'Hieland Laddie', 'Loch Lomond' and 'Comin' through the Rye'. The tunes are produced by a mechanism of hammers striking bells. Some have

seen this as the ultimate in Scottish kitsch and I suspect that the mechanism is disengaged these days to protect the mental health of the workers, but I think it an interesting feature of a distillery that has much to offer in the way of incidental interest.

The grounds were always meant to be a feature of the aesthetic whole. The pond at the front of the distillery, which now contains a fountain, was originally intended as a curling pond. The gardens were beautifully laid out with rockeries and a fantastic array of topiary art, in which shrubs and bushes magically take the shapes of familiar objects, such as stills, worm coils, bells, birds, thistles, cones and even houses. At the back of the distillery, the Achvochkie Burn has been dammed, forming a small lochan. By the side of this there is a dram safe containing a bottle of whisky and a canister, which is suspended on a rope for drawing fresh water from the dam. The luckiest visitors are thus served with a memorable dram at the dam.

Allied maintained the site in reasonable condition, employing a gardener to look after the grounds, but they had very little interest in opening it up to public view. Now it is owned by Pernod Ricard, who, as part of the takeover deal, lost Glen Grant and its famed gardens. It may not be part of their long term plan, but, if they had a mind, Tormore, with its amazing gardens and grounds, could easily become the new Glen Grant. It has great potential, especially as it is the first distillery visible on the Whisky Trail coming north from Aviemore.

As for the product, the new-make is amazingly smooth and light, no doubt thanks to the purifiers on the stills (another Glen Grant connection). Most of Tormore's 3.5 million litres of annual production goes into blending. It was long the fingerprint malt in the Long John blend. It has also featured in Ballantine's and Stewart's Cream of the Barley. The proprietary bottling of the malt is the fine, elegant 12 year old expression with its sweet, soft, aromatic, slightly nutty (toasted almonds) character. There is also a 15 yr old at 46 per cent abv, which was released by Allied. In that, the almonds have gone over to putty and play dough with a bit of afterburn on the palate. These are redeemed, however, with a drop of water.

I was with a group of Swiss friends in Ballathie House, Perthshire recently, and one woman in the group was keen to find a whisky to her taste. Nothing she had tried up to then had been acceptable to her. Maybe it was the idea of a distillery lying halfway between the Loch of Gold and the River of Pearls, but I got her a Tormore 12 year old from the bar. She was very soon nodding her approval and asking me to write down the name of the whisky. I wrote, 'Tormore — the most approachable of all whiskies.'

THE HEILAN' HILLS

Traditional

The Hielan' hills are high high
The Hielan' miles are long
But Hielan' whisky is the thing
To mak a body strong.

She'll tak a glass — be ne'en the waur
An' maybe she'll tak twa
An' if she should tak six or five
What business that tae you.

Her cuttie pipe is no that bad
To warm a body's nose
And Hielan' whisky is the thing
To paint it like the rose.

DUFFTOWN

Dufftown is the self-styled Malt Whisky Capital of Speyside,
and indeed of Scotland. It lies nestled between the hills where the
Dullan and Fiddich rivers come together. Originally called Balvenie
(like the castle), the town was founded in 1817 by James Duff,
fourth Earl of Fife.

THE BALVENIE
CONVALMORE
DUFFTOWN
GLENDULLAN
GLENFIDDICH
KININVIE
MORTLACH
PITTYVAICH

Photo: William Grant & Son

THE BALVENIE

CLOSE TO GLENFIDDICH and Balvenie distilleries stand the ruins of Balvenie Castle, which dates from at least as far back as the 13th century. In 1460, King James II restored Balvenie castle to the ownership of Margaret Douglas (the Fair Maid of Galloway). Her first husband, Sir William Douglas, eighth Earl of Douglas, was thrown out of a window at Stirling Castle by James II. She then married William's brother Sir James Douglas, ninth Earl of Douglas, last of the 'Black Douglas' line. James kept niggling the king because of what had happened to his brother and eventually he was attainted and had his estates forfeited; a divorce followed soon after. King James, moved by Margaret's beauty, granted her and her third husband, John Stewart, first Earl of Atholl, the castle for an annual rent of one red rose, to be paid on the feast of the nativity of John the Baptist (24 June) — but only if asked for!

Balvenie sits between its sister distillery, Glenfiddich, and the shell of Convalmore distillery, very close to the Dufftown terminus of the recently revived Keith-Dufftown Railway. Balvenie was constructed by William Grant in 1893 and the original distillery incorporated a derelict mansion house called New House of Balvenie. The distillery started production with second-hand stills from Lagavulin and Glen Albyn.

I was shown round Balvenie by the affable David Mair, dressed in his kilt as usual, in the very week that Balvenie opened its brand-new visitor centre. Balvenie is a much smaller distillery than Glenfiddich and its approach to welcoming visitors is different. Space is very limited and the Balvenie tour, which is by arrangement, can only take up to eight people at a time. There is a charge (Glenfiddich is free), but then the tour includes a vertical tasting of six of the Balvenie expressions. The tasting is held in the pleasantly reappointed Excise office, which is very agreeably furnished with the work of award winning furniture maker, Paul Hodgkiss.

Balvenie still has its own maltings, though (like most distilleries with floor maltings) it supplies only a proportion of its own needs. A batch of whisky using only its own malt has been distilled as an experiment, though what will happen to that batch is not yet known. The barley arrives at Balvenie and spends two days in the steep followed by six days on the floor. Finally it is moved to the kiln, where it is dried for two days; on the first day anthracite and peat are burned and on the second day anthracite only. Peating is still very light at 2 or 3ppm. The peat smoke is introduced in the kilning process by burning peat in a small, specially designed furnace with a thin flue feeding into the main furnace updraught. On the Balvenie web page, you can read coppersmith Dennis McBain's account of working in the maltings back in 1958, when he first started with the company.

In Gavin Smith's book, *Whisky Men*, Dennis describes his work as the company's coppersmith. In his opinion, the considerable difference between Balvenie and Glenfiddich whisky is down to the size and shape of the stills. Balvenie's four wash stills and five spirit stills (three of which were installed about seven years ago) are bigger than those in Glenfiddich and Kininvie. The stills are all boil ball type, though the wash stills have two slightly different shoulder shapes. Very little else is different – the barley is more or less the same and Balvenie's water source, like the others', comes from springs in the Conval Hills, though not from the famous Robbie Dhu spring.

The Balvenie seems richer and sweeter than Glenfiddich and the range of expressions includes the Founder's Reserve 10 year old, the Double Wood (matured in bourbon wood for most of its 12 years, before being transferred to Oloroso sherry casks for up to one year), the Single Barrel (a 15 year old at 50.4 per cent abv) and the 21 year old Port Wood (bourbon maturation followed by six to 12 months in port pipes).

I happen to have a soft spot for single cask whisky and almost anything with a port finish, but it is the much more affordable Double Wood that is becoming the standard bearer of the range. I found it clean and fresh on the nose with

some orange zest, spice and chocolate. The taste is very balanced — lip-smacking and long with lots of sweetness and just the right amount of sherry flavour and fruitiness. Balvenie won no less than six gold medals in the 2006 International Spirits Challenge, so it must be doing something right!

SCOTCH DRINK (Extract)

Robert Burns

Food fills the wame, an keeps us livin;
Tho' life's a gift no worth receivin',
When heavy-dragg'd wi pine an grievin;
But oiled by thee,
The wheels o' life gae down-hill, scrievin,
Wi rattlin glee.

CONVALMORE

IF YOU ARE ENERGETIC enough to walk the Dufftown spur of the Speyside Way then, as your tired limbs bring you in sight of the first buildings on the northern edge of Dufftown, you will see on your left a traditional stone-built distillery with a single pagoda. It looks closed. There are the faint remains of large white letters on the slate roof. If you look really hard and long, the name can just be made out — Convalmore-Glenlivet.

Convalmore distillery was commissioned by the Convalmore-Glenlivet Distillery Co in 1893. It was designed by Dufftown architect Donald McKay and began production on 19 February 1894. In 1904 it was bought over by W. P. Lowrie & Co (a leading broker and supplier to James Buchanan) for £6,000, with a separate deal for the whisky stock. When Lowrie retired the following year, it became part of the Buchanan empire.

Lowrie started a considerable programme of modernisation, much of which was undone when a spectacular fire broke out on 29 October 1909. The malt barn, the mash house, the tun room, the kiln and the mill were all destroyed. Fortunately it was covered by insurance and in the resulting rebuild the opportunity was taken to install some experimental equipment.

This involved fitting patent stills instead of the usual pot stills — not to make grain whisky, but to make malt whisky. This seems to be an idea which comes round every once in a while. In the 1860s, a number of distilleries were using patent stills to produce malt whisky, with 730,000 proof gallons of the stuff produced in 1864. At least two of the distilleries visited by Barnard (Cameron Bridge and Yoker) were doing this in the 1880s. And the North of Scotland Distillery produced some patent still malt whisky in the early 1960s.

Anyway, in the case of Convalmore, the spirit produced was not at all popular with the blenders so, in 1915, the column stills were removed and pot stills brought back in. This must have seemed a bit of a shame at the time as the patent stills were able to produce 500 gallons of malt spirit an hour. In 1925, Buchanan's became part of the Distillers Company Ltd. Convalmore carried on producing malt for the Buchanan blends for decades. Then, in 1964, two further stills were added, doubling the capacity. In the 1970s, the warehousing was extended, the mash house was replaced and a dark grains plant was installed to deal with the effluent from a number of distilleries.

As we know, slump often follows boom, and Convalmore was another victim of the 1980s closure programme, being put to sleep by UDV in 1985. In 1990 it was sold to William Grant and Sons, who were interested in its warehousing space as it is very close to their Dufftown complex. Grants dismantled the dark grains plant in 1995 and all the

distilling plant has been removed. It is extremely unlikely that Grants will ever reopen Convalmore.

Diageo retained the licence and the stocks and have the right to release bottlings of the single malt if they wish. This they have done in recent years, with a 24 year old (Rare Malts series) and a 28 year old, both at cask strength. By all accounts these are excellent drams, though I have not yet had the pleasure of trying either.

FROM THE *ELGIN COURANT AND COURIER*, 2 NOVEMBER 1909

Late on Friday night a very disastrous fire broke out at Convalmore Distillery, Dufftown, belonging to Messrs W. P. Lowrie & Company, Limited, Bothwell Street, Glasgow. The distillery, which is situated close to the railway station, was the only one in the district which had started work, and the fire will, of course, put a stop to the distilling operations for some time. The fire was first observed about midnight in the vicinity of the tun-room, and it quickly spread to the malt barns, and before assistance was obtained these buildings, it was evident, could not be saved. All the help obtainable in the vicinity was utilised, but this was confined to the residents in the near neighbourhood, as the townspeople of Dufftown for the most part only learned of the fire on Saturday morning. Apparatus belonging to the distillery was brought into use, but the excessive heat, it is stated, rendered the pipes practically useless, and the workers had to fall back on the use of buckets for carrying the

water, which required much more energy, and was attended with not a little personal danger. All the help available was requisitioned to subdue the flames, and by great efforts and considerable risk of life, the fire was kept from spreading to the still-house and the store adjoining the tun-room. For some time the fire raged with extraordinary ferocity, and fears for the safety of the whole building were entertained. While it was at its height the flames rose to between 30 and 40 feet high, and the scene in the valley was a remarkable and never-to-be-forgotten one by those who witnessed it. The fire lighted up the surrounding hills and threw a lurid glare into the sky. To add to the other discomforts, snow commenced to fall, and the effect of the burning building on the white landscape provided a striking picture.

The buildings which have been destroyed are the malt-barn, tun-room, kiln, mill, and mash-house. In the tun-room were six fine new vessels, only recently erected at a cost of nearly £200. In the malt-barn were six or seven hundred quarters of barley, which have been completely destroyed. This building was a splendid double-roofed one of about 50 yards long, and it has been completely burned out, only the bare walls remaining. The other places mentioned were for the most part gutted.

The origin of the fire is not known, but it may have been caused by the fusing of the electric wires, the building being equipped with electric light among its many other modern fittings.

The damage is stated to have been anything from £5,000 to £8,000. It is the largest fire that has ever occurred in the district, and the scene, a very desolate and ruined one, with nothing but the walls of the burned buildings standing, was visited by large numbers of people during Saturday and Sunday.

The distillery had only recently undergone expensive repairs, and, had the fire spread to the still-house, which contained a charge of spirits, the result would have been much more serious. The bonded stores are intact.

DUFFTOWN

DUFFTOWN DISTILLERY LIES on the southern edge of the town, squeezed into a tight little spot between the Dullan Water and the side of a hill. One of the most popular, interesting and picturesque walks in Dufftown goes by here, taking in wildlife, waterfalls and unusual rock features. The beauty of this stretch of the Dullan has impressed some interesting people: Alfred Barnard said, 'the Dullan... contains same fine bits of scenery, including the "Giant's Chair" and the pretty little cascade called the "Linen Apron", with its surrounding drapery of waving foliage', while Queen Victoria, in *More Leaves from the Journal of a Life in the Highlands* (1884), said, 'There is some pretty scenery, particularly on the Dullan about the "Giant's Chair", and at the small waterfall called the "Linen Apron".'

Dufftown distillery is very close to these features. The Giant's Chair (like the Giant's Cradle, a little upstream) is a natural rock feature carved by the power of the river. The Linen Apron is a waterfall, and earns its name when the river is in spate. The river here is very impressive, with water thundering over the 'intak' weir. Salmon can be seen leaping and the river is said to be teeming with trout. It was a study of this section of the Dullan Water that led scientists to conclude that the growth rate of salmon and brown trout is faster downstream of distillery cooling water discharge points.

The giant fish in the Dullan may be what attract the kingfishers that grace the Dufftown 15 year old Flora and Fauna series. They may also have attracted the large cats reported in this location. In 2002, a woman walking her dog by the Giant's Chair saw a 'light brown cat about the same size as her German Shepherd' walk across the path in front of her. The cat, which had a short smooth coat and a long tail with a white tip, was completely oblivious to her and seemed to be stalking something in the bushes.

Two years earlier, a night shift worker at Dufftown distillery had gone to check the water intake when he saw something running towards him. At first he thought it was a deer, but then he realised it was an enormous cat chasing a rabbit. The cat had a brown speckled coat and a large black tail with a white tip. It was about the size of 'a very large dog'. Experts think these sightings suggest a lynx, a cat which was once native to Scotland and may have either survived in remote places or been secretly re-introduced. It does seem that whisky is involved; either it helps grow the giant fish that attract the cats, or else whisky drinkers are simply more likely than most people to report seeing giant fish and enormous cats.

This is also a giant and enormous distillery, with an output capacity of four million litres. It doesn't look that impressive, tucked away in its wee corner, but appearances can be deceptive. It is true that there is an even bigger distillery nearby, but Dufftown is probably the biggest of all the Diageo distilleries and about the twelfth biggest distillery in Scotland.

Its origins are slightly obscure. There is some evidence that in 1895 the provost of Dufftown, John Symon, was keen to get involved in the whisky boom and planned to build a distillery at or near this spot. It was to be called Glenrinnes-Glenlivet. Provost Symon owned a meal mill on the site and had it converted to a distillery. The work began in 1895 and was completed the next year. Two other characters were involved from the start; Peter MacKenzie and Richard

THAT'S BIG

TOLD YOU

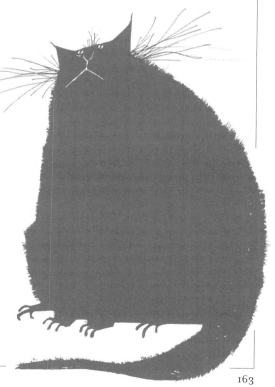

Stackpole. Peter was born in Glenlivet but had operated in Liverpool as a wine and spirits merchant for some time. In 1882 he had taken over Blair Athol distillery, so he had considerable experience. He brought with him the Liverpudlian Stackpole and the Dufftown-Glenlivet Distillery Co was born.

About a year later, the name changed to P. MacKenzie & Co (Distillers) Ltd and it appears that Symon was now no longer involved. MacKenzie, with his distilling interests and his Liverpool trading links, built up a considerable business supplying blended hooch to the Americans. That was fine until the rascally Yanks decided to ban the booze in 1920. Prohibition hit MacKenzie's company hard and when the recession also kicked in, he was forced to sell up. In 1933, Arthur Bell & Sons Ltd took over both of MacKenzie's distilleries. Bell's paid only £56,000 for the two distilleries and all the stock. They concentrated their efforts on whacking up production at Dufftown to provide the backbone malt for their blends.

Apart from a period of wartime closure from 1941 to 1946, the distillery was a steady workhorse. After the wars, some expansion was possible. In 1968, the closure of the maltings allowed the number of stills to increase from two to four, doubling capacity. A further two stills were added in 1979, though this was a bit of a squeeze and the still-house is one of the most cramped anywhere. Dufftown now has 12 stainless steel washbacks and a rather unusual Vickers mill. In 1985, Bell's was acquired by Guinness, soon to become United Distillers and eventually Diageo. The vast majority of the spirit produced goes into Bell's and other blends.

The single malt has not been easily available for a while, though that has now changed with the recent promotion of the Singleton of Dufftown. It has a gentler character than the product of the sister distillery at Mortlach, which shares the same water supply and is considered delicate, fragrant and flowery on the nose and sweet and smooth to taste; a versatile dram that can work any time, any place.

Back in the 1970s, when I was a student, it was quite common as a single malt and the 8 year old was regularly to be found on my desk as a study aid. I remember sharing a bottle with one of my lecturers, Hamish Henderson, after a session in Sandy Bell's pub one afternoon. It seemed to be a definite aid to lucid thought and spirited communication, though as the level in the bottle went down, it became harder and harder to control the flow accurately into the glasses. I think they managed to solve that problem with later adjustments to the bottle design.

ON GUID SCOTS WHISKY
(Extract)

George Bruce

O, Whisky! muckle's on ye said,
Sair on yer back abuse is laid;
Nae doubt ye're a mischievous jade,
*   Whan frien's, owre free,*
Hae been wi' ye, a fell sair head
*   Ye often gie.*

GLENDULLAN

GLENDULLAN WAS THE LAST (1897) of Dufftown's famous 'seven stills'. As a matter of fact, Pittyvaich and Kininvie were added in the 20th century, making a total of nine, but nothing stands still for long in the world of distilling. In Dufftown, the River Dullan runs into the Fiddich. Mortlach is on the Dullan just before the confluence, but Glendullan, despite its name, is on the Fiddich, just after it.

Glendullan actually consists of two distilleries. The first was built in 1897 by William Williams & Sons of Aberdeen. It was built to produce 150,000 gallons of whisky a year and the first batch went into bond on 30 April 1998. Williams amalgamated with Macdonald Greenlees Ltd in 1919, and in 1926 become part of DCL, now part of Diageo. With nearby Mortlach, it shared a private siding to the Great North of Scotland Railway. Originally, water was piped from the river for mashing, cooling and motive power, and Glendullan had a 14 feet diameter, overshot water wheel generating 16 horsepower to drive all the machinery. The wheel was still in use for some time after the Second World War, until the distillery eventually got electricity.

The earlier Glendullan distillery was re-equipped in 1962, but then, in 1972, a completely new distillery was built next door, on the field between the old distillery and the workers' houses. The new distillery had six stills, making a total of eight, and the two distilleries worked in tandem, producing very similar styles of whisky until 1985, when the old distillery was shut down. The building is still there, but is currently used for warehousing and as an engineering workshop.

The present distillery draws water from springs (including Goat's Well) in the Conval Hills. It has eight wooden washbacks (made of Canadian pitch pine) and a quite leisurely fermentation regime of 58 hours during the week and 120 hours at the weekend. Five-day working allows the copper in the stills and condensers to rest, which the distillers at Glendullan think is important. The six stills can clearly be seen through the large stillhouse windows, as their onion shapes tower above the shady course of the River Fiddich. On the side of the building, it still says 'GLENDULLAN DISTILLERY Macdonald Greenlees Ltd'. The total capacity is around 3.5 million litres per annum.

The whisky is mostly used for blending, including Johnnie Walker and Old Parr, which is a significant seller in Japan.

Glendullan was the main 'other' malt in the Cardhu Pure Malt for the brief period that controversial whisky was on the market. As a single malt, it is most likely to be encountered at 12 years old in the Flora and Fauna range, with a picture of a heron on the label. I found this a very pleasant dram, warming, sweet and sherried. I was told that Glendullan is mostly filled into second fill sherry casks and hardly ever into bourbon.

I was also told at the time of my visit that the new-make character being sought was 'clean perfume', but that for some reason it was coming out as 'nutty', so considerable efforts were being made to get it back on track. Certainly, Michael Jackson describes it as 'extraordinarily perfumy'. Glendullan was a favourite of Betty Boothroyd, the speaker of the House of Commons from 1992 to 2000. I am not sure whether she drank it or dabbed it behind her ears but some 'Madam Speaker's Order – Glendullan 12 year old', in special packaging, comes up from time to time at auction. Glendullan was also a favourite tipple of Edward VII and received a Royal Warrant in 1902. If any of the special bottles made for the king ever appeared at auction, they would be even more exciting and valuable.

THE AUTHOR'S EARNEST CRY AND PRAYER (Extract)

Robert Burns

Let half-starv'd slaves in warmer skies
See future wines rich-clust'ring rise;
Their lot auld Scotland ne'er envies,
But blythe an' frisky,
She eyes her free-born martial boys
Tak aff their whisky.

What tho' their Phoebus kinder warms,
While fragrance blooms an' beauty charms,
When wretches range in famish'd swarms
The scented groves,
Or, hounded forth, dishonour arms
In hungry droves.

Their gun's a burden on their shouther;
They downa bide the stink o' powther;
Their bauldest thought's a hank'ring swither
To stan' or rin,
Till skelp! A shot — they're aff, a' throu'ther,
To save their skin.

But bring a Scotsman frae his hill,
Clap in his cheek a Highland gill,
Say 'Such is royal George's will,
An' there's the foe!'
He has nae thought but how to kill
Twa at a blow.

GLENFIDDICH

In the world of single malts, Glenfiddich holds a special place. In 1963 it was the first company to market a single malt whisky outside Scotland, and the distinctive triangular bottle, designed in 1957 by Hans Schleger, was unleashed upon an unsuspecting world. Many people in the whisky industry, which was at that time completely dominated by blends, did not understand this move, but the company judged (and possibly shaped) the future trend of the whisky market. This vision gave Glenfiddich a head start and to this day it remains the number one best selling single malt in the world and the only one to be awarded 'Superbrand' status.

Glenfiddich, on the northern edge of Dufftown, is a very attractive distillery with a small lochan between the car park and the visitor centre and the ruins of Balvenie Castle close by. Glenfiddich caters for about 80,000 visitors a year and does so very efficiently and with care. It was the first distillery to open a visitor centre and is one of the very few that still provides a standard tour free of charge. There is also a Connoisseur's Tour for those who want a more in-depth experience with a full tasting.

The visitor facilities were improved and extended in 2005. The tour now ends in a very modern and attractive bar for a taste of Glenfiddich, and the distillery has a café, bar and restaurant (the Malt Barn), which sells good simple food as well as whisky, wine, Innes and Gunn beer and excellent coffee. This is a welcome development for the whole of Dufftown.

Glenfiddich's production water comes from the Robbie Dhu Spring in the Conval Hills. The water source gives its name to the Robbie Dhu Centre, used for tastings, events and hospitality. The year previous to my visit, I had attended an event in the Robbie Dhu Centre which was part of the Glenfiddich Artist in Residence Programme. Through this unique programme, Glenfiddich brings artists from around the world to the distillery for three months, with a remit to create new work of art inspired by the distillery and its surrounding area. The company invests approximately £100,000 each year in this valuable initiative. The company has also presented the Glenfiddich Food and Drink Awards every year since 1970.

The first spirit ran from Glenfiddich stills on Christmas Day, 1887 (the same year that Alfred Barnard's book was published). William Grant had worked at the nearby Mortlach distillery for 20 years. During 1886 and 1887, with the help of his wife, their nine children and one stone mason, he built the distillery by hand, converting his hard won savings into a project that would become a legend. Much of the original stone work still stands. Grant set up his distillery using second-hand stills from Cardhu distillery, a trick he was to repeat when he built the sister distillery of Balvenie a few years later. The Grant family still own the distillery, making it one of the very few distilleries still in the hands of a Scottish family.

As well as producing the world's number one single malt, Glenfiddich contributes to the various Grants blends. This is the biggest malt distillery in Speyside, with an annual output of around 10 million litres. William Grant might have started out with only three second-hand stills but they made fine whisky. The company currently operates 28 stills, all based on those three original styles; the wash stills are onion shaped, while one spirit still is boil ball and the other is lamp glass. The only deviation in design has been the creation of a porthole in one of the spirit stills so that visitors can see what happens inside an oper-

ating still. Glenfiddich stills are gas-fired, having changed from coal fairly recently.

To produce wash for this army of stills, Glenfiddich has two large mash tuns and 24 washbacks made of Douglas fir. The company's opinion is that wooden fermentation vessels do probably contribute in some small way to the flavour, though respect for tradition is perhaps the main reason for avoiding the use of stainless steel.

On the subject of wood, Glenfiddich has its own cooperage and regularly takes its coopers to whisky festivals to demonstrate the speed and skill of their traditional craft. Slightly less traditional is the new automated and computerised system for charring the insides of casks. Distillers have always been anxious about naked flames.

Most Glenfiddich spirit is matured in American bourbon barrels, which these days are brought over whole and not remade into hogsheads. There is also some sherry wood maturation, which accounts for about 10 per cent

of the 12 year old Special Reserve but represents a greater percentage of the other Glenfiddich bottlings, rising to about 50 per cent of the 30 year old.

The standard Glenfiddich had no age statement for a while but is now presented as a 12 year old. It is a smooth, easy-drinking single malt with not much depth but great finesse — a single malt for any time of the day but especially for sunny afternoons — sunshine, fragrant fruit and honey in the glass. A 12 year old is also available as the Caoran Reserve, which has been finished in ex-Islay casks, bringing a peatiness that might once have been more evident in the character of Glenfiddich, for example in the days when peat was the fuel throughout Speyside, or during the Second World War when coal was difficult to get.

There are two 15 year old bottlings, one of which is cask strength (51 per cent abv), while the other is the Solera Reserve, which marries three different types of oak cask. Depth of character comes through in the 18 year old, with its honey and spice, and especially in the 21 year old Gran Reserva, with its Cuban rum finish. There are various other vintages, from the 30 year old to the 1937 bottling, certainly one of the oldest and most expensive whiskies ever bottled.

The most extensive collection of Glenfiddichs in the world does not belong to the Grant family. Neither does it reside in Scotland, but rather in the Danish home of Hans Henrik Hansen. Personally, I think whisky should be drunk, not collected, but it is impossible not to feel awe and reverence when surrounded by all that dark green and black. Rare bottles of Glenfiddich are to whisky what Penny Blacks are to stamps.

Glenfiddich means 'the valley of the deer', and the red deer stag has become the emblem of the distillery. Its proud face and lofty antlers gaze out from the label of every bottle. At the time of my last visit, there was a floral display in the form of a stag, and a stag weathervane sits on top of one of the pagoda roofs. It seems appropriate that this, the most famous of our indigenous species, should be the emblem of our largest surviving indigenous whisky company.

WORLD OF WHISKY (Extract)

Robin Laing

Here's to the guys who drink the stuff
A little or a lot
And here's to the guys who sell it to 'em
What a difficult job they've got
Here's to the whisky blenders
May their noses be insured
But the guys who make it — you can take it
The keys to heaven are yours

Whisky for the heart
Whisky for the soul
Whisky stands for friendship
And stories to be told
And all around the world
Whenever whisky's poured
The hatred of the past will end at last
And peace will be restored

KININVIE

AT THE BACK OF BALVENIE stands the enigmatic Kininvie distillery. Is it actually a distillery or not? In the sense that it produces a distilled spirit, it is, but that is all it does. All the mashing and fermentation are done at Balvenie distillery next door, and the wash is piped over. Over the years since Barnard's day, distilleries have been gradually divesting themselves of many of the traditional tasks of the distiller. Very few now have their own cooperages or coppersmiths or malting, and some no longer mill their own malted barley. Perhaps this is just another logical step.

Kininvie was officially opened in 1990 by Mrs Janet Roberts, granddaughter of William Grant. Mrs Roberts' husband was a former chairman of the company. The name Kininvie was suggested by an employee in response to a competition and is the name of an estate on the east bank of the River Fiddich. Kininvie House is still there and was the childhood home of Fiona Murdoch, who ran the Whisky Shop in Dufftown for years, but it was previously the ancestral home of the Leslie family. William Marshall, the famous 18th century Scottish fiddle composer, who lived nearby, composed a Strathspey called 'Kininvie House' (and another entitled 'Balvenie Castle').

The distillery was designed to produce a different style of spirit for its blends — a somewhere between the ldich and the heavier three wash stills and six

spirit stills are designed to achieve this. At one time, people thought that the new millennium would see a release of Kininvie single malt, but so far that has not happened, and Grants have no plans to release one.

The company did, however, produce a limited edition bottling of Kininvie malt, under the name of Hazelwood. This 15 year old dram, at 105 proof, was released on 13 August 2006. The significance of all this is to do with Mrs Roberts. Hazelwood is the name of her house and 13 August 2006 was her 105th birthday. Unfortunately, the bottles, nicely packaged with photos and notes, were only made available to Grants' staff members.

By all accounts, Kininvie is a deliciously creamy and sweet whisky, but the nearest anyone can get to it is to sample some of the very respectable Grants blends. It is also a component, along with Balvenie and Glenfiddich, in the enigmatic Monkey Shoulder triple malt Scotch. The Monkey Shoulder website is worth a visit; it is quite, well, different. Monkey Shoulder is a condition, akin to repetitive strain injury, that used to afflict maltmen, due to their continually turning barley with a malt shovel. It could also be a name for the condition that would trouble anyone who tried to sample all the Monkey Shoulder cocktails, for the drink appears to feature in more of them than any other whisky.

MONKEY SHOULDER COCKTAILS

From www.monkeyshoulder.com

Blushing Monkey
Monkey Juice
Hulla Baloo
Monkey Layered on Coke
Brass Monkey
Ginger Monkey
Bitter Monkey
Monkey Mac
3 Apple 3 Monkey Sour
Monkey Martini
Monkey Fashion
Monkey Magic
Monkey 195
Monkey Bissness
Monkey Fashioned
Monkey Lover
Monkey Trailer
Citrus Monkey
Monkey Smash
Cheeky Monkey
Off the Shoulder
Monkey Business

MORTLACH

I HAVE ONLY visited Mortlach once, during the Spirit of Speyside Festival in 2005. I have, however, encountered the whisky on numerous occasions and was very interested to find out what might make Mortlach such a popular whisky, especially among blenders (it was also a favourite malt of Winston Churchill). It is only produced in limited amounts as a single malt by the owners, Diageo (mainly the 16 year old Flora and Fauna version), but it is frequently encountered in bottlings by independent companies, including the Scotch Malt Whisky Society, where I have been happy to sit in judgement upon it and where it has seldom disappointed. It is also bottled by Gordon & MacPhail, who seem to have had a particularly close relationship with the distillery over the last few decades. The oldest cask in Gordon & MacPhail's warehouse is a Mortlach from 1938.

I have had an unremarkable, very pale Mortlach from one independent bottler, which I suspect came from a rather tired cask, and I have tasted another from a port pipe which was almost undrinkable because the port cask had overpowered the whisky. Apart from those experiences, I have found Mortlach to be a very dependable and decent dram with sweet, rich, spicy notes, lip-smacking flavours and full body. From my brief visit to the distillery, it is difficult to tell what makes Mortlach such a quality dram, but there are one or two possibilities.

First, Mortlach is one of the few distilleries that still use the traditional worm tubs for cooling the spirit vapour. In worms, the condensate has a more leisurely journey through and over the copper. This is said by some to produce a heavier but superior whisky. Second, Mortlach has a relatively slow fermentation period of at least 60 hours in traditional Scottish larch washbacks. Third, and perhaps most important, are the stills; there are six at Mortlach, but they do not work in pairs as one might expect. This has come about because of the way the distillery expanded, especially in 1896. The Mortlach stills are all different but one thing they have in common is that they all have reflux bowls.

So perhaps it is the combination of reflux in the stills and the worm tub cooling, but the legend that has grown in the distillery and further afield is that the difference is made by No I still, affectionately known as 'the Wee Witchie'. In front of the still are a black metal silhouette of a witch riding a broomstick and a poster that tells us that it got its name from John Winton, a previous manager at the distillery.

John held that 'you need to have one run of spirit from No I still in every filling to give Mortlach its true character.' The Wee Witchie only produces spirit every third charge. The other two charges are 'dud runs' of feints from other stills in which the spirit is not taken off, so increasing the strength of the final run. This means that Mortlach has a unique form of two and a half times distillation. This arrangement is considered important enough that it has not been altered for generations, for fear of changing the character of a fine whisky.

The history that surrounds Mortlach is very interesting indeed. Mortlach, meaning 'bowl-shaped valley' was established in 1823. It was the first legal distillery in Dufftown, and was to be the only one for sixty-four years, until William Grant, an employee at Mortlach, left to set up Glenfiddich. Indeed, Mortlach was the first distillery in the whole Speyside area to be licensed under the 1823 Excise Act. This rather suggests that a distillery of some sort already existed at the location; this is certainly what the locals believe.

Mortlach was the site of a battle fought in 1010, in which Malcolm II defeated the Danes. The battle took place near the chapel or church of St Moluag and not far from the Giant's Chair. It was one of a series of battles between the Scottish kings and the marauding Vikings. The Scots got off to a bad start and three of their leaders were slain in the early part of the encounter. Malcolm is supposed to have prayed to St Moluag and God for victory, promising to enlarge the church if successful. The tide of battle turned and Malcolm himself threw the Danish leader, Enetus, from his horse and strangled him. The Vikings were routed and pursued to nearby Balvenie Castle, where many of them were slaughtered. Their bodies were buried in a mass grave in the castle grounds. Malcolm duly extended the church by three spear lengths.

The figure of St Moluag is a shadowy one, even compared to other Scottish saints. He is thought to have been a 6th century Irish missionary intent on converting the Picts. He was a contemporary of Columba and is reputed to have cut off his own finger and thrown it ahead of himself in order to beat Columba in a race. There are three main sites associated with Moluag, the most important one being at Lismore, the others at Rosemarkie and Mortlach. One chapel became a hospital which specialised in treating mental illness, and his name has been widely invoked against insanity. I can't imagine that that would ever have been necessary in Dufftown, certainly not since it has become such a centre of production of *uisgue beatha*, Scotland's answer to Prozac.

The Mortlach distillery was founded

by James Findlater and his two partners, Donald MacIntosh and Alexander Gordon. By 1826/27, MacIntosh and Gordon seem to have taken over. It changed hands a few times after that until it was acquired by J & J Grant, who removed the distilling equipment. It ran as a brewery for some years until John Gordon took over control in 1851 and started marketing whisky under the name 'The Real John Gordon'. Gordon was joined two years later by a partner, George Cowie, who eventually took over the reigns when Gordon died in 1867. George Cowie had been a surveyor and helped in the development of the Banffshire railway network. He was later to become provost of Dufftown.

George Cowie was the proprietor in 1886, when Barnard arrived in Dufftown. He came by train from Keith and was slightly dismayed to find that Mortlach distillery was some distance from the station. He managed to hire the only vehicle available to convey him to the centre of the village. It was 'an antiquated machine, deficient in springs and requiring renewals in several places. The horse was, however, a good one, and in less than half an hour we found ourselves at our destination, very little the worse for the jolting.'

Barnard says, 'the water used in distilling comes from the Conval Hills and the famed Priest Well, and is of excellent quality.' The Priest's Well is very close to Mortlach Church. It is said that Cowie had to fight with the owners of Dufftown distillery over water rights in the late 1890s and that there was a fair bit of clandestine tampering with water courses by the rival distillers. These days, the distilleries are owned by the same company, but water supply must still be something that requires carefully management.

The old saying goes that 'Rome was built on seven hills, and Dufftown stands on seven stills', but at the time of Barnard's visit, Mortlach was the only working distillery in the town that now claims to be Scotland's Whisky Capital. Glenfiddich was under construction but not yet on stream. Barnard described Dufftown as 'a quaint village, almost aspiring to be a town' and comments negatively on the gaol, 'a large and unsightly building', being the centrepiece of the town. That building, dating from 1839, is now the clock tower and houses the tourist information centre.

The clock itself came from Banff, where it had some notoriety in being the clock that hanged MacPherson of Kingussie. MacPherson, a rogue who stole from the rich to give to the poor, was condemned to death, and

though a pardon was granted at the last minute, Lord Braco put the clock forward so that MacPherson could be hanged before the pardon actually arrived. The episode is told in the folksong 'MacPherson's Rant':

The reprieve was comin' owre the brig o' Banff
To set MacPherson free
But they set the clock a quarter afore
And hanged him frae the tree

The clock tower, according to Gavin D. Smith in his book *The Secret Still*, was at one time used by some brazen rogues for distilling illicit whisky.

In the post-Barnard era, Dufftown went on to become a hub of distilling excellence, and Mortlach was one of the most important distilleries in the town for a long time. In the whisky boom of the 1890s, a new still-house was built, doubling the capacity from three stills to six. Around the same time, the distillery was linked in to the Great North of Scotland Railway. It was further expanded in 1903 and by the time George Cowie and Son Ltd sold out to Johnnie Walker in 1923, it was the biggest distillery in the area. Further expansions in the 1960s and the 1990s have enabled the distillery to keep pace with the times and it is now a fully mechanised, modern distillery producing almost three million litres of spirit a year for the Johnnie Walker blends.

I was served a dram of the 16 year old Flora and Fauna Mortlach at the distillery. It was kept in the fridge and the distillery worker claimed that it goes well with ice. This distillery has saintly connections, its water is drawn from the Priest's Well and its barley granary was once used as a Free Church, yet it also has a still called the Wee Witchie. When the pagan and the priest come together and Heaven and Hell combine in one glass, fire and ice may well be the appropriate combination.

THE DEIL CAM FIDDLIN' THROUGH THE TOON (Extract)

Robert Burns

The Deil cam' fiddlin' through the toon,
And he's danced awa' wi' th'Exciseman,
And ilka wifie cries: — 'Auld Mahoun,
Ach, I wish you luck o' the prize man!'

The Deil's awa', the Deil's awa',
The Deil's awa' wi' th'Exciseman!
He's danced awa', he's danced awa',
He's danced awa' wi' th'Exciseman!

We'll mak' our maut, and we'll brew our
*   drink,*
And we'll dance, and sing, and rejoice, man,
And mony braw thanks to the muckle black
*   Deil,*
That's danced awa' wi' th'Exciseman.

PITTYVAICH

THE CONSTRUCTION OF Pittyvaich in 1974 put the old rhyme about Dufftown being built on seven stills out of date, because it was the eighth. It was built on a site adjacent to Dufftown distillery by Arthur Bell & Sons Ltd, very near the ancient Mortlach Church. This was a time of optimism and expansion in Bell's, largely due to the charismatic influence of Raymond Miquel, the new chairman and managing director of the company. The distillery was built almost as a replica of Dufftown, with four matching stills, and the plan was to operate the two as one complete distillery complex. Warehousing was shared.

Pittyvaich is the name of the farm next to Dufftown distillery and was one of the names originally considered for Dufftown. The name is very old and of Pictish origin, the meaning being something like 'part of a cattle shed'. Soft water for the distillation process came from the Convalleys and Balliemore springs in the Conval Hills.

This distillery produced whisky for less than 20 years as it was mothballed in 1993. The optimism of the industry in the early 1970s became a slump by the 70s, and the 80s were a period of rabid takeovers. After closure, UDV seem to have been uncertain what to do with Pittyvaich. In 1994, experiments in producing gin were carried out there, and in 1997, new strains of barley were tested in various distillation trials. It closed down soon afterwards and has now been completely demolished. This seems a wastefully short life for a 20th century distillery and one wonders why it was selected for closure.

The first official single malt, a 12 year old, was eventually released in 1991, only two years before closure. Other independent bottlings were very rare. Michael Jackson described it as a Scottish grappa. I have tasted it, but not recently enough to remember my impressions. The few tasting notes and evaluations I have are reasonably positive, so it cannot have been closed for producing poor quality spirit.

AULD LANG SYNE (Extract)

Robert Burns

And here's a hand my trusty fiere,
And gie's a hand o thine,
We'll tak a right guid-willie waught,
For auld lang syne.

For auld lang syne, my dear,
For auld lang syne,
We'll tak a cup o kindness yet,
For auld lang syne.

GLENLIVET AND THE UPLANDS

Even higher into the hills than Dufftown are the villages of Glenlivet and Tomintoul. This is upland country; from the Cromdale Hills and Ben Rinnes, the traveller rises further towards the Cairngorms National Park and on to the very foothills of the great Grampian Mountains. The views from here are spectacular and the stories of illicit whisky-making are still fresh and real.

ALLT A BHAINNE
BALMENACH
BRAEVAL
THE GLENLIVET
SPEYSIDE
TAMNAVULIN
TOMINTOUL

Photo: Robin Laing

ALLT A BHAINNE

ALLT A BHAINNE MEANS 'Stream of Milk', perhaps because this was once a place where cows were milked, or perhaps simply because it suggests a plentiful supply of smooth whisky. Then again, it might have been chosen for mischievous reasons as it is so difficult to pronounce. The most likely correct pronunciation seems to be '*Alt a Vanya*', but I have pronounced it '*Alt a Bane*' when I wanted a rhyme and that is how it is pronounced by the people who work at the distillery.

Allt a Bhainne is four miles out of Dufftown on the road to Tomintoul. It seems quite an isolated spot and the mass of Ben Rinnes looms over it. The distillery was built in 1975 by Seagrams at a cost of £2.7m. Following enlargement in 1989, it now has a production capacity of 4.5 million litres per annum. From the outside, the building has great character, though inside it is purely functional. The architectural design seems very thoughtful and quite adventurous. It is often back-lit at night and in the gloaming it can look like a Canary Islands hotel. There are some little decorative pagodas on the roof at the western side, and the entrance porch uncannily picks out and reflects the unusual mash tun, with its canopy raised on slender pillars.

Inside the distillery, everything is open plan and the production process can be operated by one man per shift. From an operational point of view, it is one of the best distillery designs anywhere. The mill is a seven-roller Bühler, made in Switzerland. Mashing is manually operated and the mash tun's raised canopy makes it very easy to see inside; I was quite surprised to see the flailing arms of a traditional rake-stirring gear. Mashing involves four waters, which is standard for Chivas sites, apart from Aberlour. Distilling here is semi-automatic and computer controlled and the stills are quite distinctive. The two wash stills are shaped like onions with inverted cones on top and the spirit stills have long slender necks with Adam's apple boil balls — like a swan trying to swallow a curling stone. This unusual design would be intended to make a fine, light spirit and I believe the original spirit stills did not have boil balls; these were a later alteration.

It is rather difficult to know whether the design alteration worked or not as the owners have never bottled any of the whisky from Allt a Bhainne. It all goes into blends, and in particular it contributes to 100 Pipers. A few independents have bottled casks here and there, and I tried one or two from the Scotch Malt Whisky Society. A recent one, 12 years old 'honey and spice' was full of honey, caramel and orange peel on the nose while the palate had a delicious combination of chilli and toffee; it went very well with Bonnet cheese at a Society Burns Supper in Switzerland in 2007. It remains, however, a single malt with rarity value, and is even rare at the distillery as all the new spirit is tankered away to Keith for maturation. Pernod Ricard took over Chivas in 2001, and in 2002 they closed Allt a Bhainne, along with some other distilleries. Happily, in May 2005, the distillery resumed production.

I have read that the water source is the Scurran and Rowantree burns, and there is

indeed a convergence of about three burns just above Allt a Bhainne. However, in the distillery itself, I was told that the water comes from 16 springs on Ben Rinnes. It certainly comes from Ben Rinnes one way or the other, and just back down the road towards Dufftown is the most popular starting point for a walk up the mountain. From the B9009 you head north towards Milltown of Edinvillie (a charming road to drive) for a few hundred yards, and there is the car park. The track takes you up a ridge over Round Hill, Roy's Hill and the Scurran of Lochterlandoch (what a name!) on to the summit. Ben Rinnes, at 840 metres, is a Corbett.

The time I walked up, the summit was in mist and the sun was trying to break through. The sunlight threw a Brocken-spectre shadow of my body. It was very large, surrounded by a rainbow-like halo. Someday, I will return to Ben Rinnes, preferably with some friends, and have a tasting of whiskies from all the distilleries that take water from the mountain. The hardest of those to track down might well be Allt a Bhainne.

HUGHIE'S WINTER EXCUSE FOR A DRAM (Extract)

Hugh Haliburton

Come, reenge the ribs, an' let the heat
Doon to oor tinglin' taes;
Clap on a guid Kinaskit peat
An' let us see a blaze;
An' since o' water we are scant,
Fess ben the barley-bree —

A nebfu' baith we sanna want
To wet oor whistles wi'!
Noo let the winds o' Winter blaw
Owre Scotland's hills and plains,
It maitters nocht to us ava —
We've simmer in oor veins!

BALMENACH

APPROACHING SPEYSIDE FROM THE SOUTH, via Aviemore and the A9, you pass the Strathspey Steam Railway and cross the river at Grantown on Spey, where you begin to see those magical signs for the Whisky Trail. Then, just before Cromdale, there is a tiny sign, easily missed, which points to Balmenach. You have almost unwittingly crossed the border into Whisky Country!

The small village of Cromdale has a famous association with a folk song called 'The Haughs o' Cromdale'. The song supposedly describes a battle between the Marquis of Montrose and 'twenty thousand Cromwell's men': the English were roundly defeated. In fact, a battle did take place at Cromdale in 1690, when some Jacobites were defeated by government troops, and Montrose did defeat a considerable force of Covenanters at Auldearn, a few miles further north, in 1645 (as many as 2,000 Covenanters were killed). The folk song, however, confuses the two battles and ends in a Jacobite victory which never really happened. Such is the power the songwriter has to reinvent history for the popular imagination.

Sir Robert Bruce-Lockhart reminisces about his Balmenach childhood in his book *Scotch*. He tells the story of how his great grandfather, James McGregor, a farmer at Balmenach, was visited by an Excise officer in 1823. After seeing around the farm, the Excise officer inquired about one outbuilding and was told it was the peat shed. He quietly said, just before leaving, 'If I were you, Mr McGregor, I'd take out a license for yon peat shed.' James McGregor took the hint and Blamenach distillery was licensed in 1824.

The idea of illicit distilling clearly intrigued Alfred Barnard, and the first thing he did on arriving at Balmenach distillery was to ask the son of the founder to show him the 'haunts of the smugglers'. McGregor junior, clearly an accomplished storyteller, duly obliged and showed Barnard various caves and bothies, regaling him and his companions with one or two rather fantastic smuggler tales. Barnard was obviously impressed and waxed lyrical about Balmenach, even uncharacteristically mentioning the whisky — 'we tasted some 1873 Whisky and found it prime, and far superior in our opinion to old Brandy.'

Barnard was also impressed by the 'picturesque old pot stills' in the 'ancient distillery' and by James McGregor's assurance that 'for no consideration would he change a thing'. I was shown round by the distillery manager, Dennis Malcolm. Dennis, who worked for many years at Glen Grant distillery, has a family connection with Balmenach, as his wife is the great-great-granddaughter of James McGregor. Like McGregor, Dennis seems to be a man who values the traditional ways of distilling. He clearly has a pride in the Balmenach distillery, which he has lovingly brought back to production, after Inver House bought it from UDV in 1997 in a fairly run-down and cannibalised state.

Throughout its history, Balmenach has been a traditional, old-fangled type of distillery, slow to embrace progress. Barnard found everything driven by water power and uses words like 'quaint', 'old-fashioned', 'primitive' and 'ancient' to describe what he saw. An oil engine was installed in the early 1920s and electric power only arrived around 1937. Even in the 1950s, the malt mill was still being driven by steam. Dennis Malcolm refered to the place, rather affectionately, as a 'time capsule'.

Barnard announced that Balmenach was about to have a tramway built to link it to Cromdale station. In fact, that did not happen until 1897, and the initial Aveling Porter steam locomotive was replaced in 1936 by a pug engine, which continued to work there until the Beeching cuts of 1968. The puggie was always well looked after and survived at Balmenach until it was gifted in 1977 to the Strathspey Steam Railway Museum, where it still resides.

At the time of my visit, Balmenach's sister Speyside distillery, Speyburn, was undergoing a programme of automation. Dennis joked that a propelling pencil is the most automated thing at Balmenach. Having said that, he is a man of vision and described his dream for transforming Balmenach into a more attractive, better laid-out distillery with a facility for visitors in the grand but derelict house next door. Once upon a time, Balmenach had a large, Saladin box malting facility. That ceased work in the 1980s, though the buildings still stand. Consequently there are large parts of the plant that could be demolished to open the place up. At the moment, the owners are not keen on this investment, so Dennis, who is to retire in three years, may not see his dream come true.

Dennis started his whisky career as a cooper and he gave me a quick lesson in the art of coopering; how to identify dump hoggies from sherry hoggies and methods of tracking casks. His philosophy of leaving things the way they are means that he is happy with the old cast iron mash tun with its plough and rake mechanism, and with the Oregon pine washbacks. The cracks and crevices in the wood make them difficult to clean or sterilise, but Dennis is convinced that the added bacterial influence, along with the slower rise and fall of the temperature, somehow gives better body to the wash and the final spirit.

The stills at Balmenach are of the boil

ball type. One of them has an interesting brass collar, which was made and engraved when the new still was displayed in Hyde Park in 1977 as part of the Queen's Silver Jubilee celebrations. It was then almost forgotten about until Dennis found it in a store and had it polished up and replaced in time for Her Majesty's Golden Jubilee in 2002. A special edition of 25 year old Balmenach whisky was produced at that time.

Not surprisingly, Balmenach spirit is cooled in traditional worm tanks rather than condensers. Burn water fills the tanks and the spirit descends by gravity through almost one hundred metres of copper pipe, whose diameter reduces from 36mm to 8mm over its length. This additional, unhurried 'conversation' between the spirit and copper adds to the whisky's elegance.

Water for the mashing and other production requirements comes from springs in the Cromdale Hills and is piped to the distillery. Dennis is concerned that global warming is resulting in less snow in the winter months, and water supplies are now occasionally very low. Perhaps the scarcity of water is the reason that casks are filled close to natural strength at 68 per cent. Various types of cask are filled and the distillery has three traditional dunnage warehouses on-site. Between 80 and 90 per cent of the output goes for blending.

When Inver House purchased the distillery from UDV in 1997, it came with hardly any stock. Inver House can therefore produce a 10 year old malt in 2007 or 2008. At the time of my visit, I was given a preview of this in the form of a 6 year old sample from a first fill sherry cask. It was definitely coming on nicely and I could easily agree with Barnard that it was superior to old brandy. I think this will be one to look forward to.

Note: since my visit to Balmenach, Dennis has been tempted back to his old love, Glen Grant, which is now under the ownership of Campari.

THE HAUGHS O' CROMDALE
(Extract)

Traditional

The Grant, Mackenzie and MacKay,
As Montrose they did espy,
Turned and fought most valiantly
Upon the Haughs of Cromdale.

The MacDonalds they returned again,
The Camerons did their standard join,
MacIntosh played a bloody game
Upon the Haughs of Cromdale.
The Gordons boldly did advance,
The Frasers fought with sword and lance,
The Grahams they made the heids to dance,
Upon the Haughs of Cromdale.

The loyal Stewarts, with Montrose,
So boldly set upon their foes,
And brought them down with Highland blows
Upon the Haughs of Cromdale.
Of twenty thousand Cromwell's men,
Five hundred fled to Aberdeen,
The rest of them lie on the plain,
Upon the Haughs of Cromdale.

BRAEVAL

INSIDE THE CAIRNGORMS NATIONAL PARK, by the village of Chapel-town of Glenlivet, sits Braeval, at 1,165 feet (355 metres) the highest distillery in Scotland. The air here is crisp and clean and cool — almost Alpine. In hot days of summer it must be like heaven, but the winter holds sway here longer than in other parts of Speyside. Braeval was built in 1973. In the early 1970s there was period of expansion in the industry and the distilleries of Authroisk, Pittyvaich and Allt a Bhainne all came into service at that time. Braeval was originally called the Braes of Glenlivet but in the 1990s it was renamed (after the croft on which the distillery was built) to avoid any confusion with The Glenlivet down the road. There was apparently a previous distill-ery with a similar name (Braes of Glenlivat aka Bravael [sic]), which existed around 1825 for a year or two.

Braeval's water comes from the Preenie Well and Kate's Well, and from the Pitilie Burn out of the Ladder Hills. These hills, indeed the whole Glenlivet area, are steeped in smuggler lore. Just down the road from the distillery is a sign inform-ing the traveller that this was an area where there were many illicit stills between the 1780s and the 1830s and that here was a 'whisky road', often used by smugglers carrying contraband whisky from Speyside to Dundee and Perth. Also down the road was Scalan, the 18th cen-tury seminary for Catholic priests. The activities of this establishment had to be as furtive (and as risky) as those of the illicit distillers.

Some sources talk of 200 illegal stills, and some of four hundred, in the area. Certainly Glenlivet was thick with whisky bothies and we know that at around that time troops were stationed at Corgaff Castle, just a few miles away, to help the Excisemen in their struggle with droves of law-breaking whisky makers. The land-scape will have changed little since then and it does not take much imagination to picture scenes of clandestine activity, night journeys, confrontations, flight and pur-suit, and drunkenness.

A far cry from a smuggler's bothy, Braeval is a large distillery with a capacity of about four million litres per annum. It has a Swiss Bühler mill and six stills, hav-ing increased the number twice in the 1970s. The four spirit stills are of the

Milton ball or reflux bowl type. The distillery is computerised and automated and can be operated by one man. It is an attractive, whitewashed building with a decorative pagoda roof, and can look quite stunning in its setting.

Braeval has been mothballed since July 2002 and when I visited it had the melancholy atmosphere of a silent plant, but it certainly seemed that the whole distillery was intact and my impression was that it could probably be started up within 24 hours if the need arose. Chivas Brothers reopened Allt a Bhainne in 2005, but what with their recent acquisition of Allied and current levels of demand, the future of Braeval remains uncertain.

There are no warehouses on-site, just a filling bay. All the spirit was tankered away to the Chivas warehouse sites in and around Keith and Aberlour. There has never been a proprietary single malt, with almost the entire output going into the Chivas blends: Chivas Regal, 100 Pipers etc. There are, however, occasional bottlings by independents. I have sampled a good half-dozen of them with colleagues on the Scotch Malt Whisky Society tasting panel. They were from both sherry and bourbon casks, and one had been finished in a port pipe, with ages ranging from 14 to 24 years. They all tended to taste sweet, often balanced by dry pepperiness. Recurring aromas were fudge, marzipan and coconut. Certainly interesting enough to regret the lack of a steady supply of single malts from Braeval.

SCOTCH DRINK (Extract)

Robert Burns

Thae curst horse-leeches o' th' Excise,
Wha mak the whisky stills their prize!
Haud up thy han', Deil! ance, twice, thrice!
There, seize the blinkers!
An bake them up in brunstane pies
For poor damn'd drinkers.

Fortune! If thou'll but gie me still
Hale breeks, a scone, an whisky gill,
An rowth o' rhyme to rave at will,
Tak a' the rest,
An deal it aboot as thy blind skill
Directs thee best.

THE GLENLIVET

'WE SHALL NEVER FORGET our ride of 20 miles to Glenlivet on a bright spring day... up mountain roads, across highland moors, and past old Benrinnes, standing out like a mighty giant against the clear sky, the scene changing at every turn of the road like a bit of fairyland, until at last we came in sight of Glenlivet.' Barnard's poetry was inspired by the road to Glenlivet.

I travelled there in autumn and took a different road but the effect was similar. I left Dufftown travelling on the Tomintoul road. As the road climbs steadily, you become aware that this is a true Highland road. You pass the rugged bulk of Ben Rinnes on the right and feel the barley lands of Moray are falling away behind you. This is a frontier land where the meadow gives way to the moor and the ploughed field to hill-grazing and shooting estates. The ballads of these parts tell of the wild Highlanders coming down to harry the douce farming folk in pursuance of feuds and grievances or to steal livestock and women.

Glenlivet was the place where the licensed whisky trade started. The Duke of Gordon managed to convince the government that the way to suppress illicit distilling was to make legal distilling more attractive. This led to the Excise Act of 1823, which allowed smaller scale production under licence. George Smith of Glenlivet was the first to apply.

He was not popular among the smugglers as a result of this, and had to carry a pair of pistols, given to him by the Laird of Aberlour, for protection. He was required to use them on at least two occasions when smugglers were intent on 'doing him in'. Those pistols are still on display in the distillery. George Smith must have been a brave man. In any event, he knew what the future held for whisky and that the days of the peat-reekers were numbered.

George Smith had started out as an illicit distiller himself, at his farm at Upper Drumin. Glenlivet whisky already had a fabulous reputation, even before licences were introduced. King George IV famously asked for it by name in 1822 on his royal visit to Scotland. Smith's legal distillery was licensed in November 1824, and production first flowed early in 1825. Within a year he was producing a hundred gallons a week. In 1827, he complained to the Board of Excise about the continuing threat of violence from illicit distillers and smugglers. Within months, the authorities responded by sending a garrison of troopers to Corgarff Castle. Thus began a determined effort to quash the smuggling trade in the area. Also in 1827, Smith's business almost failed on account of capital debts and a drop in sales. The Duke of Gordon gave him financial help to see him through, and by the 1830s, production was up to 500 gallons a week.

Twenty years later, George Smith could not meet the demand from his small distillery at Upper Drumin, so he built a new one in 1859 at Minmore, just a few hundred yards down the glen. This new site was a much grander and more efficient plant

than the old one, with a potential output of 4,000 gallons a week. It has been the home of The Glenlivet ever since. A cairn and a plaque stand on the lonely site of the original distillery, which lies close to the path of the Speyside Way.

George Smith died in 1871, and when Barnard arrived at Glenlivet in 1885 the proprietor was George's younger son, John Gordon Smith. At that time, John Gordon had recently been through a costly court battle to prevent a growing rash of distilleries adopting the Glenlivet name and benefiting from the reputation his family had built. The result of that court case was that only 10 distilleries had the right to suffix their name with 'Glenlivet' (Barnard attaches it to five distilleries) and only Smith's could be called 'The Glenlivet'.

Barnard comments on the 'numerous teams of magnificent horses' and 'magnificent stabling'. The Speyside railway had reached Ballindalloch in 1863 and Glenlivet was certainly using it to reach its markets in London and beyond, but, in order to negotiate the seven or so miles between the distillery and the railway, it was necessary to employ the horse and cart.

Needless to say in such an upland area, Barnard describes a kilning process that is 'fired principally with peat,

WHEEST

which is of fine quality and dug in the district.' Nowadays the phenolic content of the malted barley is 6ppm, which, though probably far below normal 19th century levels, is a touch higher than most present-day Speyside distilleries. In 1890, just a short time after Barnard called, the distillery was seriously damaged by a fire and some of the buildings had to be renovated.

John Gordon Smith was a member of the 6th Volunteer Battalion of the Gordon Highlanders and became a colonel. In 1899 he sent a cask of Glenlivet to the Gordon Highlanders during the siege of Ladysmith in South Africa. In 1886 Barnard said of him, 'the hospitable proprietor is a true highlander, and not only entertained us and our driver, but invited us to spend our next vacation with him, and have some days grouse shooting on a fine moor of about 10,000 acres'. It is tantalising to imagine how Barnard's group was 'entertained' — he says nothing about tasting the whisky — and indeed one wonders whether he ever took up the invitation to do a bit of shooting.

Glenlivet distillery is a survivor. It has had its difficult patches, not only in the early days. Demand and therefore production fell dramatically in the first decade of the 20th century. John Gordon Smith died in 1901 and ownership passed to his nephew, George Smith Grant, but George died in 1914 and his eldest son, John, was killed in France in 1918. John's younger brother, Bill, who had been twice wounded and decorated for bravery in the war, took over the reigns. He needed all that bravery to drag the company back to health. It was not until Prohibition ended in the USA in 1933 that the company's fortunes began to turn.

Bill Smith Grant had the vision to concentrate on the US market and, at a time when everyone was interested in blends, he saw a future for single malts and pushed The Glenlivet tenaciously. By 1964, half of all single malt sold in the US was Glenlivet. In 1952 it amalgamated with Glen Grant and in 1970 these two tied up with Longmorn to form The Glenlivet Distillers Ltd. That company was purchased by the Canadian company, Seagram, which had already purchased Chivas Brothers in the 1950s.

The distillery now produces about 3.5 million litres of whisky each year. Mashing at Glenlivet involves four infusions and the fermentation takes place relatively quickly at 42–48 hours in eight Oregon pine washbacks of some antiquity. There are eight stills of the lampglass design, which are among the tallest in Scotland. One of these has a viewing porthole on the side, which is a fascinating thing to peer into when a distillation is taking place. Distillation is computer controlled. The distillery ran out of cooling water last year for the first time ever. Both of these things are signs of the times, but while we can control the technology of production, the climate is just a bit beyond our power.

Though this is the second best selling malt worldwide, a considerable amount of Glenlivet still goes into blends (about 60 per cent). There are various ages, wood finishes and vintages of the single malt. At the moment, my greatest praise goes to the Glenlivet Nàdurra, a 16 year old, cask strength (57.2 per cent) batch bottling, which has no caramel or chill-filtering (Nàdurra means 'natural'). The colour is bright yellow gold and the nose gets a blast of aromatic oak, which in a few minutes turns to vanilla, pineapple and sherbet lemons. A hint of tobacco leaf stops it from becoming too airy-fairy. A dessert whisky with a substantial kick.

At the time of my visit, I sat in the distillery savouring a dram of the French Oak (eleven years in sherry wood, one year in new French Limousin oak; sweet, rich and spicy) and watching the weather. It was a contemplative moment, wondering all sorts of things: why do distilleries still mill the malt instead of buying in grist?; why do they still have padlocks on the spirit safes? etc. The sky was divided in battle lines, blue skies to the north and storm clouds to the south, where the mountains lay. I was lucky to be travelling back to Dufftown and into the blue. The road was deserted and it was downhill all the way — hard not to slip into the persona of a rally driver!

I have tasted many expressions of Glenlivet, but the greatest impact was when I was given a taste of 40 year old (distilled 1964) by Ian Logan of Chivas at the Whisky Fringe in Edinburgh in August 2006. It was a really intense, penetrating dram with continuous waves of rewarding flavour, like winning a jackpot on some flavour fruit machine — and fruit was the key, like fresh air blowing at you across a heavenly and exotic fruit punch (pineapple, banana, aromatic pear, peaches and passion fruit). I swear there was musk in there, too. The palate was rich fruit and spice with iced coffee. The finish stayed with me all the way home. The night sky was clear and I settled back in the garden to watch dozens of Perseids shooting across the IMAX screen of the sky. I shall always associate that special experience with that special whisky. Thank you, Ian.

OLD RHYME

Glenlivet it has castles three,
Drumin, Blairfindy and Deskie,
And also one distillery,
More famous than the castles three.

OLD BANFFSHIRE SONG
(Extract)

Nae dose o' drugs is half sae guid
To clear the brain or cleanse the bluid;
It does for physic, drink and fuid —
The guid auld Glenlivet Whisky O!

FHAIRSON SWORE A FEUD
(Extract)

William Aytoun

Fhairson had a son
Who married Noah's daughter,
And nearly spoilt ta flood
By trinking up ta water.
This he would have done —
I at least believe it —
Had the mixture been
Only half Glenlivet

OLD TUNE

A fiddle tune, 'Glenlivet Whiskey Highland Strathspey', which is also known as 'Minmore Schottische', was written by J. Scott Skinner, the Strathspey King, who was born in Banchory, Kincardineshire, in 1843. The tune appeared in the Elgin Collection of 1884 and the following anonymous verse is sometimes printed with it:

Scott Skinner made anither tune,
The very dirl o't renched the moon.
Till ilka lassie an her loon
Commenced to dance fu frisky-o.

SPEYSIDE

SMALL DISTILLERY – BIG SCOTCH

DESPITE THE NAME, there are those who would consider Speyside distillery to lie outside the area of the Speyside whisky region. Certainly it is remote from the rest, but in my opinion it has more right to be considered a 'Speyside' than some of the others which claim that title. For one thing, it is closer to the river than most of them. It lies near the point where the River Tromie runs into the Spey. The Spey is visible from the distillery, and when it floods it comes to within a hundred metres.

The actual location is called Drumguish (the 'g' is practically silent) and is reached by a road that runs from Kingussie past the forbidding ruin of Ruthven Barracks. The road runs by Drumguish before continuing to Kincraig and Coylumbridge and finally looping on to Aviemore. The actual source of the Spey is about 20 miles away in the Monadhliath Mountains, so it is already an established river by the time it picks up the Tromie. The distillery uses the water from the Tromie, which, with its source in the high Gaick Forest, is probably about as pure as you can find anywhere.

There was a previous distillery nearby, also called the Speyside distillery. That was built by the MacPherson-Grants in 1895 and survived only until 1911. The MacPherson-Grants also built Newtonmore and Tomatin distilleries. Of the three, only Tomatin survives, becoming, at one time, the biggest malt whisky distillery in Scotland. The present incarnation of the Speyside distillery, on the other hand, is one of the smallest, at about 500,000 litres annual capacity.

In 1955, George Christie bought Old Milton House at Drumguish, with a view to building a single malt distillery. Thirty-five years later, the first spirit flowed from the stills, so Speyside is the result of a cherished dream and a project that took a long time to mature, just like a good whisky. Back in the late 1950s, George converted a brewery at Cambus to create a grain whisky distillery and the North of Scotland Distilling Co, so he was already making whisky somewhere else while the Speyside project inched forward. George and his son, Ricky, made the dream come true, but they are no longer directly involved in the company.

The building at Speyside distillery is interesting. It is an extension and conversion of an old mill, with lade and wheel still very much in evidence. The work was carried out by Alex Fairlie, a dry stone dyker, who almost single handedly worked on the project off and on for 25 years. A plaque on the wall attributes the building to him. Some of the stone is local and some came from the demolished buildings at the famous Aberlour Orphanage. Alex had to extend the building in a dog-leg because of the proximity to the lade, which gives it a rather unique shape. There are still holes in the walls, into which Alex fixed horizontal fence posts to support his makeshift scaffolding.

Andrew Shand is the distillery manager. His father was the manager at Longmorn distillery and Andy grew up in the grounds there. He himself started out at Glenlivet and worked in various Chivas Brothers distilleries before becoming master distiller at Ben Nevis. As he showed me round, Andy was able to tell me stories from other distilleries, as well as the complete history of Speyside. I asked him about a large sign I saw lying in a corner. It said 'Lagganmore Distillery' and I learned that Speyside is the film double for the fictitious Lagganmore distillery, featured in the BBC's *Monarch of the Glen*. That programme is watched by many millions of people in the UK and in North America, so Speyside may well be the most visible of all the distilleries in Scotland, though it was news to me as I live in a television-free environment.

There were only three or four mashes completed at the end of 1990. After 25 long years in the construction, it seems there was a bit of a rush to get some spirit produced in 1990, as the stencils for that year had already been made. I had been introduced to the 1991 Speyside (61.1 per cent abv) by Ricky Christie. It is bottled under the Scott's Selection label (the company bottles a number of whiskies under two independent labels; Scott's Selection, which are unchillfiltered, cask strength whiskies, and Private Cellar, which is bottled at 43 per cent abv). Scott's 1991 Speyside is a beautiful, mouth-filling, breath-taking dram; the nose has lemon, eucalyptus and geranium and the palate is liquorice root and nippy sweeties. I was sorry to see the bottle finished and could identify readily with the poem which appeared on the company's website (see below).

The single malts produced are the no-age-statement Drumguish, which is a younger brother to the flagship The Speyside (10 and 12 years old so far, and a 15 year old to come). The 12 year old, in colour and in smell, evokes whin bushes on a summer's day and the flavour is bar-

ESTIMATED TIME OF COMPLETION 25 YEARS THANKS · ALEX ·

ley sugar, with apricots in the after taste. The company produces a number of ages of a whisky called simply 'Speyside', but these are blends. There are also one or two vatted malts, such as Glentromie. The stills were designed to fit into the existing space, so they are not very high, yet they produce a very light, clean, drinkable new-make spirit with a definite aniseed flavour. There are plans to do some highly peated runs at around 60ppm, so the future looks interesting.

Whisky from Speyside distillery is bottled by a Danish company as Cu Dubh ('Black Dog'). This is Speyside whisky with the addition of so much caramel that it looks black — a successor perhaps to the now collectible but never drinkable Loch Dhu. Speyside is also a component in the whisky liqueur Cock o' the North. More scandalously perhaps, it was whisky from Speyside distillery which was sold by the cask, under the name of Grandtully, by the aptly-named Stephen Jupe, to many unsuspecting investors in the 1990s. Jupe misled investors about the returns to be expected in purchasing casks and, after an investigation by the Serious Fraud Office, was convicted in 2004 and sentenced to five years in prison. The owners of Speyside distillery were not aware of what Jupe was up to and were in no way involved in the fraud.

A TRIBUTE TO SPEYSIDE

Anon (thanks to Ricky Christie)

We are sitting tonight in the fire glow,
Just you and I alone,
And the flickering light falls softly
On a beauty that's all your own.

It gleams where your round smooth shoulder
From a graceful neck sweeps down;
And I would not exchange your beauty
For the best dressed belle in town.

I have drawn the curtain closer,
And from my easy chair
I stretch my hand toward you,
Just to feel that you are there.

And your breath is laden with perfume,
As my thoughts around you twine,
And I feel my pulses beating
As your spirit is mingled with mine,

And the woes of the world have vanished
When I've pressed my lips to yours;
And to feel the life blood flowing
To me is the best of cures.

You have given me inspiration
For many a soulful rhyme —
You're the finest old Scotch Whisky
I've had in a long, long time.

TAMNAVULIN

IN 1994, WHYTE & MACKAY (subsidiary of Jim Beam Brands) took over Invergordon Distillers. Within a year they had closed three malt distilleries — Bruichladdich, Tullibardine and Tamnavulin. Since then, the first two have been sold on and have reopened with considerable success. Tamnavulin is a bit on the large side and not very pretty, so there it sits, like the shy girl at the dance that no one asked up on the floor. The distillery is classified as 'mothballed', is maintained wind- and water-tight, and the equipment has not been cannibalised. For six weeks in 2000 it was put back into production, but it has been silent since then.

Invergordon Distillers Ltd built Tamnavulin in 1966. In 1994 it was taken over by Whyte & Mackay, and in 2001 Whyte & Mackay was sold by Fortune Brands to a new organisation, Kyndal, in a management buyout. In 2006, the Whyte & Mackay range was relaunched with a confident makeover. Depending on what happens to the fortunes of the company and its brands, there is a possibility that Tamnavulin could be brought back into service or sold in the next year or two. The company talked about bringing it back into production in 2005, but nothing happened. After 10 years of closure, the cost of breathing life into Tamnavulin should not be underestimated.

There is little of romance about Tamnavulin. The name means 'mill on the hill' and there is still evidence of a mill here (once used for carding wool).

The old mill was eventually put into service as a very attractive visitor centre at Tamnavulin and actually stayed open for two or three years after the distillery ceased production. It is the only pretty, traditional-looking part of the complex and has even had its water wheel restored. The distillery is only yards from the River Livet and still has an attractive picnic site, near the old mill. Of all the distilleries that have ever called themselves '-Glenlivet', Tamnavulin is the closest to the actual river, and that includes the one still known as The Glenlivet. However, Tamnavulin dropped the suffix in 1990.

The rest of the distillery is functional and utilitarian and it represented modern production practices in its day, though it was never fully automated. The annual capacity at full production from the three pairs of stills was four million litres of fairly light, fragrant and floral malt. Some was destined for the various Whyte & Mackay blends, and much would have been exchanged on reciprocal arrangements, though I am told that the main destination of Tamnavulin in recent years has been good quality, economy single malts, many of which were bottled under various made-up names for supermarket chains, e.g. Ben Bracken, which was sold by Lidl in some quantity. The extensive warehousing, steel-racked, 12 casks high, would have held a veritable lake of the stuff. In the 10 years since Tamnavulin stopped production, the single malt has often been seen on the shelves at a very good price. That seems to be changing now, which suggests that the stock is running low.

The big question for Tamnavulin is what the future might hold. It is a large distillery and was probably not very cost-efficient to operate. It would take a lot of money to bring it up to modern standards. Against that, it has the advantage of being reasonably self-sufficient, with its own warehousing, draff driers, pot ale evaporators and effluent disposal systems. The future is uncertain, but single malt fans will be pleased if it survives. Too many decent distilleries have been cast loose to float down the river of memory into the endless ocean of obscurity.

MORE THAN JUST A DRAM (Extract)

Robin Laing

*Take clear water from the hill
and barley from the lowlands,
take a master craftsman's skill
and something harder to define,
like secrets in the shape of copper stills
or the slow, silent, magic work of time.*

*When you hold it in your hand
it's the pulse of one small nation;
so much more than just a dram,
you can see it if you will —
the people and the weather and the land,
the past into the present is distilled.*

TOMINTOUL

THE GENTLE DRAM

THE VILLAGE OF TOMINTOUL, currently home to about 300 inhabitants, is the highest in the Highlands (Wanlockhead, down south in the Lowther Hills, is the highest village in Scotland). The area, once under the stewardship of the notorious Wolf of Badenoch, has always been a rather wild and remote land, beyond civilisation and the law. Following the defeat of the Stuart cause at Culloden in 1746, the government decided there was a need for military roads to allow access to these unruly parts. In the 1750s, therefore, a road was built linking Corgarff Castle and Fort George. Tomintoul lies on the course of that military road.

It was set out as a planned village between 1775 and 1780 by the Duke of Gordon. The plan was that the villagers could make a living from cultivating lint and spinning linen yarn. However, that seems not to have been successful and the inhabitants relied on casual labour and the illegal production of whisky, much of which was sent down to market along those very military roads. In 1792, the local minister reported that every one of the 37 families in Tomintoul sold whisky, and drank it too. Queen Victoria, no doubt scouring the Highlands for decent drams, declared that Tomintoul was a 'tumbledown, miserable, dirty-looking place'.

Because of its position, Tomintoul has always been a stopping off point for travellers and, due to its good and plentiful whisky, it has developed quite a reputation for hospitality. Nowadays it is very much geared towards tourism and I would be surprised if any latter-day tourists would echo the harsh judgment of Queen Victoria.

Tomintoul distillery actually lies about five miles north of the village, in Strath Avon, between Glenlivet Forest and the Hills of Cromdale. It was built in the modest whisky boom of the 1960s by Hay & McLeod and W. & S. Strong (two firms of whisky brokers and blenders in Glasgow), and the first spirit ran from the stills in July 1965. About 10 years later, it was acquired by the Scottish Universal Investment Trust and subsequently became part of the Whyte & Mackay stable, until it was sold to Angus Dundee in 2000. Angus Dundee is a London based firm, which has built its operation and reputation mostly through the supply of bulk blends to supermarkets and other outlets throughout Europe. It is under the control of the Hillman family. In 2003, Angus Dundee also acquired Glencadam distillery in Brechin.

The location of Tomintoul distillery was chosen mainly for the pure spring water from the Ballantruan Spring. The high altitude (at 268m, it is one of the three or four highest distilleries in Scotland) can cause difficulties in terms of access. Everyone is familiar with the frequent closure of the Cockbridge to Tomintoul road due to snow. During the winter phase of construction, the contractors always had two weeks' worth of building materials to hand in case they were cut off from the outside world. Purpose-built braziers enabled work to proceed even in the coldest weather. The distillery was designed to have a large barley storage capacity (200 tonnes) for the same reason.

The people who built this distillery wanted a supply of Speyside single malt for their blends and were after a whisky of light character. For that reason, they chose very tall stills (almost as tall as Glenmorangie's) with boil balls and ascending lyne arms for greater reflux. The number of stills was increased from two to four in the 1970s. The older stills, though they have probably been replaced a number of times since then, still retain their riveted collars, whereas the newer ones are welded, with a brass ring over the weld. Despite the size of the stills, it is the still-house that represents a slight bottleneck in the production process. Nonetheless, the annual output capacity is 3.2 million litres, which is quite high for a distillery with four stills.

There are other interesting aspects of production at Tomintoul: one of the largest mash tuns around; heat recovery systems in some of the condensers, contributing to the evaporation of pot ale; the Koch Membrane filtration plant, which can remove copper from effluent and spent lees (it is the only distillery on Speyside with this kind of plant). However, perhaps the most interesting and unusual bit of plant is what distillery manager Robert Fleming calls 'the Blending Tank Farm'. This is a facility

that allows Angus Dundee to make a huge range of blends and other products, to meet the specifications of a variety of customers. The Farm has 10 holding and blending vats, which allow the company to respond quickly to orders. Robert told me how one customer wanted a new blend the next day, and staff at Tomintoul were able to respond.

Various other things help Angus Dundee to react with imagination and versatility to these bulk orders. For example, there is a huge stock of maturing spirit on hand. Present stock, in palletised warehouses, amounts to 78,000 casks. Two new warehouses will soon add a further capacity of 36,000 more casks. Stocks go back almost to the first year of production; certainly they have some from 1966. A considerable part of the spirit produced here is exchanged in reciprocating deals for other malts and for grain whisky, which is needed for the creation of blends. Only about 2 or 3 per cent of the output is currently bottled as Tomintoul single malt (though much more goes into customers' own-brand malts). However, that may change in the future as the three main expressions of 10, 16 and 27 year olds become established (the 27 year old won a double gold medal at the San Francisco World Spirits Competition).

The company has recently reviewed its wood policy and has taken steps to access sherry casks from a bodega in Spain. In addition, twice a year for the last four or five years, Tomintoul has been making a heavily peated spirit from 60–65ppm malted barley. This allows it to give a range of character to the blends, but in addition it has recently been bottled and released as Old Ballantruan. This is a welcome addition to the Speyside range and represents the second peated Speyside to come onto the market after Benriach; interesting times.

I have to confess that of all the Speyside areas I visited, it is the upland area that I fell in love with the most. Tomintoul is marketed as 'the gentle dram', but the land and the weather, at times, are not so gentle. This is the only distillery I ever visited where I saw a tractor with a snow plough attached. There is a photo on the wall, taken by Robert Fleming, of casks standing with a good eight inches of snow on top. Robert comes from a family with a tradition of at least four generations of distillers associated with Glenlivet. A harsh land and climate might produce a gentle dram, but it produces interesting people; people who work hard and play hard, who take everything seriously, including their fun – and who value hospitality very highly indeed. That could be another reason why this village had such a reputation for it.

I visited Tomintoul in the autumn, when dappled sun and showers created a dynamic of water and light on the high road into the Cairngorms National Park. The harvest here seemed different – tall trees were being logged and a sign told of peat cutting operations. Incredibly, I passed a field of sunflowers, and had to stop to take a photo. I later discovered this was a food crop for pheasants. The car park at the distillery was populated by ducks and the roads were full of pheasants. This place is a paradise for photographers and other wildlife. I hoped it would not be long before I could return.

As to the whisky — the 10 year old is nutty and putty-like with Madeira honey cake, vanilla, lemon and straw; fruity but with a solid heart. The 27 year old, on the other hand, has sherry, plums and oak sawdust, along with melon skins and fag packets. The Old Ballantruan is a 50 per cent abv, smoky Speyside that makes you cry for what we have lost but hopeful for what we might regain. I like them all.

FAREWELL TOMINTOUL

Traditional

Farewell Tomintoul! for the hour's come at last
When I can only think of the joys in the past,
For destiny bears me away from the glen
Where dwell bonnie lasses and true-hearted men.

What though in their spite petty minds have decried thee,
And said with a sneer they could never abide thee!
I am sure that in this I shall not be alone
When I say I am certain the fault was their own.

As for me, I can say, with my hand on my heart,
I'm as loath as can be from Strathavon to part;
Its hills and its streams and its valleys shall be
Ever dear as the home of my childhood to me.

I have found hospitality, kindness and truth
To be deeply engraved on the hearts of its youth,
And I know you can always with safety depend
On them aye standing true in the cause o' a friend.

I shall always remember with happiness deep,
Criaghalky, Knocklochy, and Ailnaic so steep,
The clear, winding Avon, the fair Ellan-no,
And the birk-covered braes that surround Delnabo.

Starthavon, farewell! though I cannot remain,
I trust that thy vale I may visit again;
How that will delight me, words fail me to tell,
But soon may the day come — Strathavon, farewell!

ABERLOUR TO TOMINTOUL

Matt Armour

*Aberlour to Tomintoul, thirty mile as the
    corby flees
But yon wee bit of travelling has brought strong
    men to their knees.
It's no' the steps you're taking that will rob you
    of your might
But Aberlour to Tomintoul is a hell of a
    Saturday night.
Yes, Aberlour to Tomintoul is a hell of a
    Saturday Night*

*Wullie McPhee he liked a drink: no man had
    seen him drunk.
To get blootered, bladdered or paralysed was a
    thought he'd never thunk.
When the beast cam' tae his heid, by the full
    moon's shining light,
He found that Aberlour to Tomintoul was a
    hell of a Saturday night.
Yes, Aberlour to Tomintoul is a hell of a
    Saturday night.*

*Phemie McPherson did nae harm, in her hale
    natural life.
Her lips had never touched a dram, neither as
    maid nor wife.
When aff the wagon she did cowp, losh what an
    awfy sight,
For Aberlour to Tomintoul is a hell of a
    Saturday night.
Yes, Aberlour to Tomintoul is a hell of a
    Saturday night.*

*You're looking a bittie puzzled; gie'ing me a gey
    queer look,
Forcing me tae jalouse that you've never read
    the book
The ABC of whisky, cornucopia of delight,
That makes Aberlour to Tomintoul a hell of a
    Saturday night.
Yes, Aberlour to Tomintoul is a hell of a
    Saturday night.*

INDEX OF DISTILLERIES

SOME CDs BY ROBIN LAING

One for the Road
(Greentrax 313)

The Angels' Share
(Greentrax 137)

The Water of Life
(Greentrax 246)

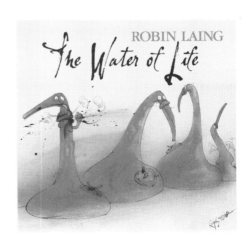

The Whisky Muse: Scotch whisky in poem and song

Robin Laing

ISBN 1 946487 95 0 PBK £7.99

Whisky – the water of life, perhaps Scotland's best known contribution to the world. *Muse* – goddess of creative endeavour. *The Whisky Muse* – the spark of inspiration to many of Scotland's great poets and songwriters.

Brought together by Robin Laing, a highly respected Scottish folk-singer and songwriter, and based on his one-man show *The Angels' Share,* it combines two of his passions – folk song and whisky. Each poem and song is accompanied by fascinating additional information, and the book is full of interesting tit-bits on the process of whisky making.

Reflected in these poems and songs are the pleasures (and medicinal benefits) of imbibing this most beloved of spirits as well as the unfortunate consequences of over-indulgence, the centuries of religious disapproval, the temperance movement and the exciseman.

The stories told here are lubricated by warmth and companionship, best enjoyed with a dram in hand. Slainte.

This splendid book is necessary reading for anyone interested in whisky and song. It encapsulates Scottish folk culture and the very spirit of Scotland.

Charles MacLean, Editor at Large, WHISKY MAGAZINE

This excellent little book collects together all the best Whisky songs [and poems] in Scotland and presents them alongside Bob Dewar's witty cartoons.

SCOTCH MALT WHISKY SOCIETY NEWSLETTER

One of Scotland's premier folk singer-songwriters.

SUNDAY POST

Statistics, opinion, handy wee hints are deftly slipped into his writing, precisely the sort of thing useful in a blether over a dram or two.

SCOTS MAGAZINE